How to Become a Dynamic Biblical Preacher

How to Become a Dynamic Biblical Preacher

A Manual for Pastors and Laypersons

JOSEPH B. ONYANGO OKELLO

Foreword by Ralph Partelow

WIPF & STOCK · Eugene, Oregon

HOW TO BECOME A DYNAMIC BIBLICAL PREACHER
A Manual for Pastors and Laypersons

Wipf & Stock
An Imprint of Wipf and Stock Publishers
199 W. 8th Ave., Suite 3
Eugene, OR 97401

www.wipfandstock.com

PAPERBACK ISBN: 979-8-3852-1360-3
HARDCOVER ISBN: 979-8-3852-1361-0
EBOOK ISBN: 979-8-3852-1362-7

VERSION NUMBER 060424

Scripture Quotations taken from the Holy Bible, New International Version, Copyright 1984 by International Bible Society.

To
Geneva Methodist Church for allowing God to shape you
through the preaching of his word.

Contents

Foreword

THE AUTHOR OF THIS book, Joseph Onyango Okello, was one of my homiletics students in a Kenya Bible College three decades ago, who showed remarkable promise then in his studies and especially in preaching. I taught a method of preaching that was sort of a mix between the "Big Idea" method used by Norman Vincent Peale (past pastor of Marble Collegiate Church in New York City) and Haddon Robinson (president of Denver Seminary in Denver, Colorado). I was not surprised when Joseph became so proficient in preaching and teaching as he continued in his career and ministry because he had mastered this method early on in his studies at our college. What is written in this book he has written from his own vast experience and will no doubt be extremely helpful to those who are beginning their practice in preaching as well as to those who are already experienced in the art. Using this "Big Idea" method in communicating God's Word will both help the preacher and the listener to retain the content of the message for the benefit of both. I am joyful and honored, as Joseph's former teacher, to have had a part in his training in Kenya and to be a small part of this effort to follow the encouragement of St. Paul to Timothy: "And the things you have heard me say in the presence of many witnesses entrust to reliable people who will also be qualified to teach others" (2 Tim 2:2).

Dr. Ralph Partelow
Arizona

Chapter 1

The Task Ahead

THE CHRISTIAN WORLD IS hungry for good preaching. It is hungry for preaching the listener can remember, one the listener can repeat. Have you ever walked out of a service wondering what the preacher, that day, was trying to say? I have. That kind of thing happens either because the preacher was ill-prepared for preaching or because the preacher did not present the message in a way the audience could remember. Good preaching challenges the audience to take positive action toward the right spiritual direction consistent with the word of God—preaching that can be remembered and re-preached by the listening audience.

The purpose of this book is to help shape you, the reader, into a good preacher. By a good preacher, I refer to the ability to present the word of God in a way that will make any audience listen to you. Every preacher I know wants their audience to listen to them. No preacher I know takes it well when a member of his audience sleeps, surfs the web, or reads a newspaper throughout his sermon. They want members of their audience to listen to them, and they express their disappointment and, sometimes, their anger that someone failed to pay attention to the sermons they preached.

I have developed and used the preaching method I describe in this book for over thirty years. The first person to introduce me to this method was my college preaching professor, Dr. Ralph

Partelow. However, when I first sat under his tutelage, I resisted this style of preaching because I thought it was too westernized for my taste. It was Western because it seemed too linear to appeal to the non-Western mind. Things changed at some point, though. The more I learned how I could incorporate illustrations peculiar to my culture, the more I began to embrace the method. It worked so well that I found myself embracing it even more. I did not have to abandon my ethnic identity to use this method. I could actually incorporate my identity and remain culturally relevant as I present the gospel.

I used the method throughout my pastoral ministry. Every time I was on the pulpit, members of the audience were ready with pen and paper in hand. I noticed how they took copious notes of what the sermon was all about. Throughout the week, a significant number of my church members testified how they shared that Sunday's sermon with their friends. It was clear to me that they listened to the sermon, they learned the sermon, and they went out and gave lectures on the sermon.

When I relocated to the United States of America, I continued to apply the homiletical principles I learned at Scott Theological College. They have remained a part of my preaching style to this day. For sixteen years, I was the pastor of Duncan Chapel, Jimtown United Methodist Church in Lexington, Kentucky. In the first three of those years, I used this preaching method religiously. I then returned to Kenya for a year as the senior pastor of Africa Inland Church, Jericho, in Kenya's capital city, Nairobi. I used the same method of preaching there, and then returned to Duncan Chapel, in the United States, retaining the same method.

Consistently, without fail, I received good reviews from my listeners. At no time have I received negative comments about the preaching style I have adopted for the years gone by since learning the method I wish to share with you in this book. I believe I got the opportunity to be elected the president of Kenya Christian Fellowship in America because of how the gospel came to members of this organization based on the preaching method I have retained throughout my preaching career. It is the method I describe in this book. For some reason or other, the method I endorse throughout this book, when used correctly, presents the word of God in a way that exposes the audience to listen to the voice of God through the conduit of the preacher.

I said, above, that the comments I received from my listeners while using this method have consistently been positive. This is true. I have received negative comments, however, on how I have pronounced words or confused some biblical stories on the pulpit. These negative comments were not because the method I have always used is faulty. Rather, they came because I failed to pay attention to the facts as I was presenting them, and since the method kept the audience quite captive, they were attentive enough to detect my error in presenting the facts. I note that this happens to any preacher, and merely underscores the importance of remaining alert throughout the preaching event from start to finish. Hence, the criticism did not come because of poor methodology, but from incorrect facts.

My promise, as you read this book is very simple: if you apply the principles outlined in this book consistently, you will be a dynamic preacher. In other words, you will present the word of God in a memorable and repeatable way. Your audience will remember the gist of your sermon and will be able to repeat the gist to those who wish to know what your sermon is all about. The goal of this book is to turn you into an effective preacher of the word of God. An effective preacher is a powerful preacher who, through the use of the method outlined in this work will succeed in getting any audience to listen to him, or to her.

As you work through the principles delineated in this work, I will expose you to ways in which you can present your material in a memorable way. By this promise, I imply that once your audience hear you preach, they will, in turn, be able to preach to that fellow member of your church who failed to show up for service for whatever reason. At the very least, a good sermon should be memorable, and a good sermon should also be re-preachable. It should be captivating enough for those who hear it to be able to preach it again.

In my thirty years of preaching, I have tried to present my sermons in ways I would hope my hearers could re-preach them. This outcome is really one of the joys of preaching. After waiting on God to give you the right word over a certain period of time, and you take the trouble to put that word before your congregation in a way they can understand and even restate, you experience deep gratification. I believe this outcome of repeatability qualifies as a mark of good preaching. Hence, good preaching is both memorable and repeatable. Of course, some bad sermons are also memorable and repeatable. Hence repeatability and memorability are not the only marks of good preaching. We will still need to add more items to that list, such as biblical fidelity and explanatory power.

So, welcome to the world of preaching. I will walk you through the process by sharing what I do in terms of initial preparation for the preaching event. This revelation could come as a surprise to you. But if you are the sort of person I suspect you are (an interested preacher-in-the-making), this revealed secret should not surprise you. It should be something you should find intuitive, or reasonable. From the preparation stage, I will then take you to the delivery stage. Both stages are important and should not be ignored.

One of the biggest mistakes wannabe preachers make is neglecting to prepare their sermons. I will say more about this, of course, in the coming pages. But preparing for the preaching event is absolutely crucial for the overall task of ministering from the pulpit. It is analogous to preparing physical food. No one really wants to eat uncooked food that one would, ordinarily, need to cook before eating. Eating raw beef, for example, puts you at risk of ingesting harmful bacteria. Similarly, unprepared preaching is dangerous preaching. It can bring untold spiritual suffering to the congregation. Hence, adequate preparation is important in the sense that it helps one avoid the sorts of errors one would make when unprepared. Therefore, if you are ready to join me in this journey, let me invite you to turn the page and walk with me. Bon voyage!

Chapter 2

Preparation of the Heart

WHERE DOES ONE BEGIN to find resources for sermon preparation? I will let you into a secret. This secret about the first step toward preparing to preach could come to you as a surprise. Preparation begins with the person of the preacher. The person commissioned, invited or called to preach even one sermon must be prepared in heart and mind. A prepared heart is just as important as a prepared sermon. Perhaps you have been doing this already over the years. Rejoice! You have the first step nailed. Just the same, one of the most important starting points for a prepared heart is in the prayer closet during your personal devotion.

One well-known preacher made a comment during a radio broadcast in one of his sermons—a comment that made a lasting impact on me for years and still does. He said, "God is more interested in the heart of the minister than he is interested in the ministry of the minister." His reason for making this claim was very simple and, surprisingly, quite correct. He said, "The reason God is interested in the heart of the minister is because God knows if the minister's heart is set right, the ministry will go right." This preacher could not have been more correct in his observation about the prepared heart of the preacher.

I know of no better way to prepare your heart, as a minister of the word of God, than to have a daily quiet time with the Lord.

This habit is crucial. I have used it for decades in my preaching ministry, and it has never failed in preparing me for the preaching ministry. Exactly how this happens will become clear in the next few pages. I suspect, though, that one reason your minister chose you to preach for him is because he possibly heard about your prayer life and how you take your devotions seriously. He trusted you were telling him the truth about your daily walk with the Lord, and he knew, at once, that your heart was ready for such a task. Your heart is the preparing ground for a successful sermon, for a sermon that will connect with your audience.

Whenever I walk into my prayer closet, I develop a habit of communicating with God. Communication, as you most likely know, is a two-way process. Therein you hear from God by reading his word, and you speak to God through prayer. Usually, before I open the word of God, I ask him to speak to me through the process of reading his word. During those times, I read a passage of Scripture that speaks to me either directly or indirectly. Once I sense a message coming from the reading of the word of God, I write it down, as if I am preaching to myself, which is what is actually happening at that time. In other words, I always want to preach to myself and challenge myself from the word of God before I can stand on the pulpit to deliver that message. As I write it down, I put it in a preachable format, namely, I develop the outline, which will be fully developed into a sermon later. I will say more of this later, but what I imply by this expression is the fact that I write my initial thoughts for my sermons from the reading of the word every time I go into the prayer closet. I have developed sermon outlines almost every day of my life since I started taking my devotions seriously. Once the outline is developed, writing the sermon out in full becomes relatively easier.

I am not unrealistic to note, however, that in some instances, sensing God's inspiration for preparing a sermon outline could take you up to a week or more. To be sure, this state of affairs will be the norm in many instances and stretches of your devotional hour. If no inspiration for a sermon outline comes at your first try, let this not discourage you. You will have certain days when the inspiration comes instantly. You will have other days when your desired inspiration will take time to download!

Notice the implication of this practice. Suppose you have an inspiration for a sermon outline each time you walk into your prayer closet to commune with the Lord. In one year, you could have up to 365 sermon outlines in your sermonic library. This fact played itself out in my life several years back! That number amounts to enough stock for preaching for seven years, assuming you will be preaching every Sunday without taking a break. In other words, a year's worth of devotions is enough to give you more than you need for preaching regularly as a minister of his word. The more you do this, the more God will open doors for you to deliver his word to an audience ready to listen, and very soon he will put you on a path to becoming an itinerant preacher. Your church will not be the only place you will be invited to preach or speak. Other settings will come your way and you will be surprised at how many doors God will open for you. God has done this for me faithfully, without fail.

However, let us consider the other aspect of the devotion, namely, the praying aspect. Once God has given you his word for the day, your task now is to respond to him in prayer. Many well-established ministers of the gospel encourage their followers to employ a four-stage format of praying during their devotional hour, namely: adoration, confession, thanksgiving, and supplication. Adoration includes a sense of awe and wonder toward God. It also includes worship and praise. Since many individuals do not know how exactly to go about this, I recommend selecting a song or a hymn of praise and singing it prayerfully unto the Lord. He delights in it. Confession involves taking stock of one's life throughout the day that went by and identifying thoughts, words or deeds one may have allowed to flow out of one's life in a way that dishonored the Lord. One then mentions them by name before the Lord, and subsequently asking for forgiveness. Thanksgiving involves gratitude to God for different favors that have come your way. One item you should thank God for is the word he has just given you in your time of devotion. Go back over the outline you have written down and thank God for every inspiration you have received out of reading his word. Supplication is twofold: it includes petition and intercession. In petition, you bring your personal needs before the Lord, and in intercession, you pray for others in need of God's intervention in their lives. As you pray for your personal needs, do not forget to ask God to use you to deliver the word he has spoken through you. Doing this is important because you want to bathe that word in prayer through and through. It makes a difference.

I know for sure how it feels to deliver a sermon God has anointed and to deliver one that is more of a dry, impotent lecture. Even the weakest sermon, when bathed in prayer, comes forth with great power specifically because sermons do not depend on eloquence of speech as much as they depend on the power of God. The apostle Paul speaks about this fact in 2 Cor 2:1. He writes: "When I came to you, brothers, I did not come with eloquence or superior wisdom as I proclaimed to you the testimony about God." And in 1 Thess 1:4, Paul alludes to this power when he says, "Because our Gospel came to you not simply with words, but also with power, with the Holy Spirit and deep conviction." Spending time in prayer over the word you will speak some day in the future ensures that the word itself is already bathed in prayer and will come forth with the anointing of the Holy Spirit.

One of the most interesting things about preaching in the power of the Holy Spirit is the fact that throughout the preaching event, a sermon that God has given you will be carried on the pulpit by God's anointing. And the preacher of that sermon will know it. I personally know it because I know for sure how every time I have stood on the pulpit to preach a sermon God has given me, God seems to take over the proclamation of that word, and he only uses me as a tool to convey that word. Stated differently, I find myself "taking a backseat" of sorts while standing right there on the pulpit as the word of God comes out from the preaching entrusted to me. It is as if I am there listening to that word even though I am really the one preaching it. At other times, I feel as if God is the one preaching it and he carries me along in the preaching event, just as he declares in 2 Pet 1: 21, which reminds us that the prophets of long ago spoke as they were moved by the Holy Spirit. They did not follow cleverly invented stories about God's revelation. In a sense, every time I preach a word I know I have prayed for again and again and again, I experience what Peter says in this verse because I sense God's Spirit carrying me along throughout that preaching event.

If you have not experienced this fact already, you will know what I am talking about when you begin with the heart in your preparation for the preaching event. In many ways it is an affirmation of God's approval. The danger, however, is succumbing to the lure of pride. This experience is spiritually potent, and the potency could quite easily be a source of pride for the preacher—something the preacher must always take the trouble to guard against. Pride is what got the devil expelled from heaven. Pride should not be the reason God will use to expel you from his pulpit.

At any rate, the point I want to press in this section is simply this: sermon preparation begins with the heart of the preacher at the prayer closet. The assumption here, of course, is that the preacher of the word already has an established personal relationship with the Lord Jesus Christ, and wishes to live a life of holiness unto the Lord. That is the initial baseline assumption. And this assumption is important because unsaved preachers abound, and a good number of them mislead the flock in grievous ways. The preacher of God's word should be one with a personal relationship with the Lord. In other words, he or she should be born again. Once that assumption is clear, we can then press the importance of maintaining that daily and closer walk with the Lord Jesus Christ each day. This walk includes a daily reading of God's word and a response to the reading of that word by praying through adoration, confession, thanksgiving and supplication. I recommend these as the initial stage of sermon preparation. How about we move to the next stage of helping you answer your pastor's request?

Chapter 3

Preparation from the Text

YOU ARE NOW MAKING your first move to answer your pastor's request, namely, finding a text for your sermon. Preaching from the text of Scripture is what every minister has been called upon to do. The preacher's primary source is the text. The preacher may use other sources for illustrations of a biblical text. But those sources cannot replace the text of the Bible. The Bible is where the message finds its grounding and its foundation. Churches that die often do so because they have received a steady diet of nonbiblical preaching. When you preach from the Bible, you are sure to get a hungry audience ready to feed on God's word. So, how does one begin, and how does one proceed?

One must begin by studying the text of Scripture. Study the text in different versions. Many version of the Bible exist out there. The only version I will ask the would-be preacher to guard against is the New World Translation, specifically because it mistranslates the original language in a way that severely compromises key doctrines of the Bible. For example, it introduces Jesus as a god (note the small letter *g* in the translation) rather than as God. They translate it this way in John 1:1 as follows: "In the beginning was the word, and the word was with God and the word was a god." Clearly, this interpretation compromises the deity of Christ and is not true to the rendering of the text in its original language.

A parallel Bible with multiple translations is a wonderful resource because it gives you a one-stop shopping for different textual translations of the Bible. Usually, the texts agree on the meanings of every verse in the Bible. Moreover, when the meaning of a text is unclear in one translation, a different translation often clarifies the apparent obscurity. Some of the major translations out there include the King James Version, The New King James Version, the American Standard Bible, the New American Standard Bible, The New International Version, The New Revised Standard Version, The English Standard Version and the New Living Translation. Of course, many more examples can be found out there.

Ideally, one should read the Bible in its original languages of Hebrew and Greek, which usually happens in seminaries and Bible colleges. But not everyone can go to seminary or to Bible college. Besides, some of those who go to seminary shy away from reading the Bible in these original languages. Still, we must not always overlook the importance of the original languages in our Bible studies. Whereas learning the Bible in the original languages is absolutely important, one can use different online resources to find the meaning of a given word in the Bible in its original language without having to learn that language. Of course, more dynamics go into the translation of a given text than merely looking up the meaning of a word.

Other resources that one should find helpful in studying the text include commentaries and study Bibles. Commentaries often give verse by verse explanations of the meanings of the text, helping the reader to understand the meaning of a given passage or text. Study Bibles sometimes do not go as deep as commentaries do, but having them is more beneficial than not having them. Armed with commentaries, parallel versions of the Bible, Study Bibles and concordances, one can be all set for the task of preparing for the preaching event, assuming, of course, that the would-be preacher has been preparing, as a person, for the task of preaching.

The importance of the text cannot be ignored. Besides being the word of God, one of the crucial things about the text is this: it helps to define the topic to be preached. By giving the text a deeper look than merely glancing through it, you, the preacher, can determine the topic the text in question is trying to address. The topic can be a one-word topic such as anger, love, kindness, and obedience. Or it can be a phrase such as spiritual gifts, spiritual fruit, faith in God, and loving thy neighbor. The important thing to note, here, is that the text of Scripture helps you to determine the topic to be addressed. Without a clearly defined topic, you will leave your congregation unsure of what you will be talking about. Thus, the text gives you the topic to preach on.

However, when selecting the topic for preaching, one must be sensitive to the need of the hour by selecting a relevant topic. It would seem rather odd to preach about the birth of Christ, for example, on Easter Sunday, though some preachers have somewhat forced it through! Similarly, it would seem odd to preach a funeral sermon at a wedding, or preach a wedding sermon at a funeral. One must be sensitive to the needs of the audience by knowing the particular needs of the audience and season of the year at a given time. The topic, therefore, must be relevant. Still, the point I want to emphasize here is the importance of deciphering the topic from the text.

In my first preaching event, never did I once refer to the Bible, even though the Scripture was read at the very beginning, before I actually preached. More recently, also, I had an experience where I sat through a whole series of sermons, for about three weeks, where the preacher derived his sermon from movie clips. The church was malnourished for three weeks, without hearing a sermon based on the word of God! Of course, the sermon was there, but it was not Bible-based. It was movie-based. Moreover, the sermon itself was derived from the internet, word for word! That was a perfect recipe for spiritual death in the church.

When God calls you to preach, he expects you to preach from his word. The apostle Peter warns his readers that if one's gift is preaching, one must do so as if speaking the very words of God (1 Pet 4:11). I know of no better way than to speak from the Bible— not from the *Reader's Digest* or from *The National Geographic* or from *Time* magazine, but from the Bible. I see no reason why one cannot use any of these resources for illustrating the text. But I also see no reason why anyone could use any of these resources as the primary text for preaching. Unfortunately, some preachers in a variety of so-called progressive churches are walking away from the public reading and teaching of Scripture and embracing more and more of texts external to Scripture as their source of authority.

Admittedly, some texts can be extremely difficult to use for sermons. The genealogies, for example, can be quite a challenge. Still, sermons have been built upon these texts in remarkably powerful ways. Also, when one reads some chapters in the book of Joshua (see, for example, Joshua 19), or 1 Chronicles, one will have to be a homiletical genius to squeeze a sermon out of those texts. Doing so is not impossible. It can be done, but with great difficulty. However, some of the Bible stories in Genesis, Exodus, Numbers, Joshua, Judges, Ruth, 1 Samuel, 2 Samuel, 1 Kings, 2 Kings, 1 Chronicles and 2 Chronicles can be quite inspiring. The words of the prophets of the Old Testament can also be excellent resources for preaching, provided one knows how to approach them. Approaching them directly without correlating them to texts in the New Testament leaves one vulnerable to misinterpretation.

Overall, however, I cannot emphasize enough the importance of staying as close as possible to the biblical text in seeking materials for your sermon. The Bible is your first go-to place when looking for what to say. When you begin to re-state the Bible in your own words while remaining true to the text, you are putting yourself on the path to preaching. When you begin to explain that text in a way your readers can understand, you are beginning to assume a prophetic role of teaching the word of God.

Therefore, when your pastor asks you to preach, the pastor assumes you are familiar with much of the biblical text. Your pastor assumes you know the Bible well enough to give you the invitation to stand up on the pulpit and deliver the word of God. Something about you convinced the pastor to invite you to preach. Stay close to the text of the Bible. In Chapter 8, we will look at what goes into the process of interpreting the text or, for that matter, explaining the text to your audience, and what you will need to do to make your explanation clearer. For now, however, I just want to underscore the importance of staying as close to the text as possible. The text is the key to connecting your audience with God. Pastors who know better also know that the Bible text is the key to the spiritual growth of the church. They know that the moment they walk away from the Bible in their preaching, they begin to see a spiritual decline in their church. God has not given us the option of preaching from a different resource. He has not given us the option of preaching from songs or from poetry or from famous speeches or from TV clips. He has given us the only option of preaching from the word.

Before we go into the word, I will introduce you to the structure of the sermonic process. More importantly, I will introduce you to my style of preaching. It is not the only preaching style out there. Many styles are available, such as narrative preaching. However, the preaching style I have used has never failed me. It has worked every time I have used it for several reasons: first, the audience can remember it. They can remember the key points I make in my sermon. Second, the audience can repeat it. In other words, my audience could go out into the world and re-preach the sermon just as if they were the ones putting the sermon together Third, it is a method easy to grasp. I hope, therefore, that by the time you are done reading this book, you will have been empowered to preach in a way that will bring a lasting transformation into the life of those around you, just because the pastor asked you to preach. That request might have been the most life-defining moment in your life! So, let's get going and learn how to put a sermon together!

Study the following passages and suggest a topic for each of them.

1. John 3:16

2. 2 Chronicles 7:14

3. Revelation 21:1–4

4. Isaiah 11:1–9

5. Matthew 1:17–21
6. Psalm 23

Chapter 4

The Topic and Purpose of Your Sermon

ONCE YOU HAVE SETTLED on the topic of your sermon, you need to determine what the purpose of your sermon will be. The purpose of your sermon gives your audience a reason for believing they need to sit there listening to you. The purpose of your sermon should also be as clear in the mind of your audience as it is clear in yours. You do not need to announce publicly to your audience what the purpose of your sermon is. A clear purpose is one recognized by your audience as you preach without you having to announce it publicly. It is, in a certain sense, the motive of your sermon. Once you have made the purpose of your sermon clear to yourself, most of the preparation process will begin to fall into place.

A good sermon has both a general purpose and a particular purpose. Before writing your sermon, you need to ask yourself the question: is the general purpose of your sermon to inform, to challenge, to encourage, to correct, or to educate? Notice how general these purposes are. They do not locate the identity of who will be informed, or challenged, or encouraged or corrected, or educated. They leave it open-ended. Moreover, as with the sermon topic, the sermon purpose is governed by the text to be studied. If, for example, the sermon text has a message of encouragement, then the general purpose of the sermon should be to encourage the audience in some way. If the sermon text has a message challenging the reader to some kind of action, then the general purpose of the sermon should be to challenge the audience to act in some way. If the sermon text has a message that corrects a certain kind of behavior, then the general purpose of the sermon should be to correct the audience. Similarly, if the sermon text has a message that educates the reader about a certain doctrine, then the general purpose of the sermon should be to educate the audience in a way that will empower them with knowledge.

In short, the general purpose is just that—it is general. It does not specify the identity of the audience. In this sense, it is open ended. It simply informs, or encourages, or corrects, or rebukes, or advises, or challenges, without specifying who the recipient of the exercise of that purpose really is. Once the general purpose has been put in place, the specific purpose, or particular purpose, can now come into focus. How does the particular purpose look like, and what does it entail?

Before answering this question, I will need to mention here my intention to give it a partial treatment for reasons that will become clearer later. For now, I simply mention that the difference between a general purpose and a particular purpose of a sermon is that a particular purpose is tailor-made for a specific audience. Suppose, for example you have been invited to speak to your fellow congregation members. The particular purpose will be tailor-made for that audience. Let's assume you belong to Geneva Methodist Church, in Florida. The particular purpose will target the needs of the members of that congregation.

Let's assume, then, that your general purpose is to assure. Your particular purpose will be to assure the members of that congregation of something. Let us assume, further, that your sermon text is John 11:17–44, which is the story of the death of Lazarus and how Jesus raised Lazarus from the dead. That text will not only govern your general purpose, it will also govern your particular purpose. As you read that text, you become more and more convinced that Jesus feels the grief of Martha and Mary, and you want to assure the members of Geneva Methodist Church of the same, namely, that Jesus feels their pain. This format, then, is how your particular purpose will take: to assure members of Geneva Methodist Church that Jesus feels their pain.

Suppose, then, you were writing the outline page of your sermon, which comes before the main body of your sermon. It will have the following ingredients:

- Title: "Jesus Feels Your Pain"

- Text: John 11:17–44

- General Purpose: To assure

- Particular Purpose: To assure members of Geneva Methodist Church that Jesus feels their pain.

Let me take a text from 2 Tim 4:6–8. It is the text where the apostle Paul seems to believe his life is coming to an end. Perhaps, after reading that text, you feel or think that Paul's intention is to tell the recipients of his letter that the Christian life is a challenging life. Hence, you get the impression to inform your members of Geneva Methodist Church that the Christian life is indeed a challenging life. Here, then, is how the first ingredients of your outline page will look like:

- Title: "The Christian Life"

- Text: 2 Timothy 4:6–8

- General Purpose: To inform

- Particular Purpose: To inform members of Geneva Methodist Church that the Christian life is a challenging life.

A third example can be taken from the Old Testament, and more specifically, from the book of 2 Chron 26:3–5. It is the story of Uzziah, who became king when he was sixteen years old. His mother's name was Jecoliah, and she was from Jerusalem. Uzziah did was right in the eyes of the Lord, the Bible says, as his father, Amaziah, had done. He sought the Lord in the days of Zechariah who instructed him in the fear of the Lord. And as long as he sought the Lord, the Bible says, God gave him success. Upon reading that text, you get the impression that the topic of that text is God-given success, and the general trend is to specify how God-given success came to Uzziah. Your general purpose, then, would be to inform. If you have been called to preach to members of Geneva Methodist Church, then your particular purpose would be to inform members of Geneva Methodist Church how God-given success comes or how God-given success is possible. The outline page of your sermon will, therefore, look like this:

- Title: "God-Given Success"

- Text: 2 Chronicles 26:3–5

- General Purpose: To inform

- Particular Purpose: To inform members of Geneva Methodist Church how God-given success is possible.

One of my favorite passages of Scripture is Mark 1:29–34. Simon's mother-in-law was in bed with a fever, and Simon and Andrew told Jesus about her. We are told that Jesus went to her, took her hand and helped her up. Then the fever left her and she began to wait on them. The Bible notes how that evening, after sunset, the people brought all the sick and demon possessed to Jesus, and that the whole town gathered at the door. The Bible notes that Jesus healed all who were sick with various diseases, and he also cast out many demons. However, Jesus would not let the demons speak because they knew who he was. Upon reading this text, you then see that your general purpose, while using this text for your sermon, is to encourage. The particular purpose, if you have been called to speak to, say, Geneva Methodist Church, is to encourage members of Geneva Methodist Church to bring their needs to Jesus Christ. Your outline page will then have the following items as the first ones on the list:

- Title: "Bringing Your Needs"

- Text: Mark 1:29–34

- General Purpose: To encourage

- Particular Purpose: To encourage members of Geneva Methodist Church to bring their needs to Jesus.

I have used the four examples in this section to demonstrate the difference between the general purpose and a particular purpose. The general purpose is rather open-ended, and does not specify who the target audience is, although it is based on the text of Scripture. The particular purpose is also based on Scripture, but it goes beyond the general purpose because it specifies who the sermon is targeting. More than that, it species what the sermon will accomplish after it has been fully preached. Once you have stated your particular purpose, you, the speaker, will be able to evaluate yourself to determine whether you, indeed, accomplished what you set out to do in your sermon.

I reiterate what I said at the beginning of this section: the purpose of your sermon should be clear to you, clear enough such that, upon preaching the sermon, your audience will not be at a loss about what you were trying to accomplish. Without a clear purpose, your sermon will not accomplish much, and you will have a confused audience by the end of your preaching event. You do not want your pastor to regret asking you to preach.

Tony Evans, the famed preacher from Dallas, Texas, made a comment about clarity from the pulpit. He said, "A mist in the pulpit becomes a fog in the pew." In other words, if something is not clear to you as the preacher of God's word, it will be even more unclear to those who will be receiving the word of God from you. Make sure your purpose is clear and well-articulated to yourself. This helps to give you the general direction of your sermon in a way that will put you on the path to successful preaching.

Having come this far, I still need to make an important point here. Even though we have stated the particular purpose of the sermon, what you have seen so far about the particular purpose is only partial. A full particular purpose of the sermon includes the theme and the main points of the sermon. But since we have not delved into the process of developing the theme and main points of a sermon, I leave that task for a later treatment in an upcoming section. In order to do that, we have to look at what goes into putting the theme of the sermon together. So, let's turn to it.

Exercises

Study the following passages of Scripture and describe a purpose for each of them:

1. John 3:16

2. 2 Chronicles 7:14

3. Revelation 21:1–4

4. Isaiah 11:1–9

5. Matthew 1:17–21

6. Psalm 23

Chapter 5

The Theme of Your Sermon

IN THE STYLE OF preaching I describe here, the theme of a sermon is different from the topic or title of a sermon. The theme of a sermon is a sentence that interprets, in seven words or less, the text of Scripture you will be using for your sermon. Stated differently, the theme is a sentence that teaches a doctrinal truth of a given passage in a way that makes it applicable to the lives of the audience, but it does so in seven words or less. It is a complete sentence, with a subject and a verb. Think of the theme of a sermon as the backbone of the sermon itself. It is the main idea or thread running through your sermon. I will select a few passages and demonstrate how you can derive specific themes from those passages. Whereas the title of the sermon gives an audience an idea of what the sermon is all about, the theme of the sermon helps to fulfill two goals. First, the theme tries to interpret the sermon text in one sentence. Second, it interprets the sermon text in a way that fulfills the goals and purpose of the sermon—the goals and purpose described in the purpose statement.

Perhaps you find this expression dizzying and confusing. Let me make it clearer with a few examples from the previous chapter. To save you from trying to find that chapter, let me restate the sermon text, the sermon title, the purpose statement here:

- Title: "Jesus Feels Your Pain"
- Text: John 11:17–44
- General Purpose: To Assure
- Particular Purpose: To assure members of Geneva Methodist Church that Jesus feels their pain.
- Theme: Jesus feels your pain.

Notice where the theme appears. It appears immediately after the particular purpose. Notice also that the theme is one sentence. I did say earlier that the theme is different from the title. In this example, the theme and the title are identical. But whereas most titles are as short as one word, and need not be a sentence, the theme must be a full sentence *whose main points* help you to answer the question "How?" or "When?" or "Why?"—questions which have been prompted by the theme itself. For example, when you state this theme in your sermon, you need to show *how* Jesus feels the pain of his people. I will get to that point soon.

But notice what the theme is doing. It is interpreting the entire passage of John 11:17–44 *in one sentence*. It is suggesting, based on the events in the passage, that Jesus feels the pain of his people, and it will aim to show exactly how Jesus feels the pain of his people. The theme, therefore, is drawn or derived from the passage in a way that helps to fulfill the purpose statement. Additionally, you, the preacher, decide, based on how God has spoken to you as you read the text, what the theme will be and how it will look like. Somebody else will look at that very passage and will, quite conceivably, have a different theme which, upon examination, will be just as true to the passage as the one I have given you here. In other words, the theme is true to the text, but it is also based upon how the passage speaks to you or, more accurately, how God speaks to you through that passage.

Let's try another example taken from the previous chapter.

- Title: "The Christian Life"
- Text: 2 Timothy 4:6–8

- General Purpose: To inform
- Particular Purpose: To inform members of Geneva Methodist Church that the Christian life is a challenging life
- Theme: The Christian life is a challenging life.

The fact that this theme is derived from that text of Scripture should be clear. The theme itself will be prompting the question *How?* It will prompt the question "How exactly is the Christian life a challenging life?" The main points will answer this question, which we will examine in the next chapter. Generally speaking, though, consider that Paul is discussing the fact that he is about to die, and that he has also fought the fight, finished the race and kept the faith as he anticipates his reward from Jesus Christ. The task you have, as the preacher of the day, is to delineate exactly how challenging the Christian life is. Once again, how you derive the theme from any passage of Scripture depends upon what message you understand the passage to be conveying to you or, more specifically, what message you understand God to be conveying to you through that passage. I will explain the "how" of the theme in a different section. For now, let's be content with focusing on what the theme is.

In addition, notice that the sermon title here is much shorter than the theme. The sermon title is "The Christian Life." The theme is "The Christian life is a challenging life." This also helps to illustrate another aspect of the theme, as follows: The theme is a continuation of the sermon title. In this example, the sermon title gives you the first three words of the theme, which is seven words long. In the previous example, the sermon title gives you the first four words of the theme. However, in that example, the first four words of the title are also the first four words of the theme.

A third example helps to make this clearer. Here we go:

- Title: "God-Given Success"
- Text: 2 Chronicles 26:3–5
- General Purpose: To inform

- Particular Purpose: To inform members of Geneva Methodist Church how God-given success is possible

- Theme: God-given success is possible.

The title of the sermon is "God-Given Success." The theme has the first three words of the sermon title as follows: God-given success is possible. As it stands, the theme feels incomplete. It raises the question "how" or "when"? Your task, as the preacher, will be to show exactly how or when this God-given success is possible. The sentence of the theme is a full sentence, but it leaves the thought feeling incomplete. Still, we have a theme that seems to permeate the text, and your task is to lead the congregation through the process of showing the hearer how God-given success is possible.

One more example will be helpful:

- Title: "Bring Your Needs"

- Text: Mark 1:29–34

- General Purpose: To encourage

- Particular Purpose: To encourage members of Geneva Methodist Church to bring their needs to Jesus

- Theme: Bring your needs to Jesus.

The sermon title is catchy. It almost feels like an invitation—a demand for a response. If a sermon title can accomplish that task, it makes the theme of the sermon much easier to formulate. In this case, the theme is "Bring your needs to Jesus." An audience hearing this theme proclaimed from the pulpit will be attentive enough to ask why or how one should bring his or her needs to Jesus. Once again, your task as the preacher is to help your audience know exactly how or why they should bring their needs to Jesus based on that sermon text.

Allow me to make a few more remarks about the theme. The theme should be brief enough to be remembered. The theme should not be too long to be remembered. The longest theme should be six or seven words. When it gets too long, your audience will struggle to remember it. The shorter the theme, the better. To be sure, if the theme can be as short as the title, as some of the examples have shown are, it will be more effective, and more memorable.

Second, your theme from a given text need not be identical to another person's theme from that text. Remember, God speaks to us in our different situations and how one person sees one text is not exactly the same as how another person sees the same text. That reason possibly explains why your pastor asked you to preach. Your pastor strongly suspects God speaks to you and that you hear and obey God's voice. For that reason, your pastor will confidently assign you to the pulpit to share the message God has given you.

Third, the theme may, quite conceivably, be as short as the sermon title. But it is different from the sermon title. The sermon title merely specifies the topic to be preached. The theme fulfills the purpose of the sermon in a way that the title does not, namely, by giving a specific call to action, action more fully described by the main points of your sermon.

Fourth, the questions the theme tries to answer is what helps to connect it to the main points. This may sound strange, but I will try to make it clear quite briefly, and then expand on it in the next section. Let's take the first one: Jesus feels your pain. Upon hearing this, one will ask himself or herself the question, in what way does Jesus feel your pain? Or how does Jesus feel your pain? Or how do you know Jesus feels your pain? To answer this question depends on how you develop your main points, which, in turn, depends on your understanding of the text.

Once again, your answer to this question depends upon how you read the text. Let me offer a few suggestions: Recall the text that gave us the theme, "Jesus feels your pain." The question to ask is this: how does Jesus feel your pain? As I read the text, I de- rive the following points to answer the question: Jesus feels your pain because he comes to you, because he comforts you, because he calls you, because he cries with you, because he cares for you, and because he cures you. Each reason here is based on Scripture, and in the next section I will try to show how I derive them from Scripture.

The other example runs as follows: the Christian life is a challenging life. How is the Christian life a challenging life? Once again, I derive my points from the text in order to answer that question, as follows: The Christian life is a challenging life because we have a price to pay for it, we have a part to play in it, and we have a prize to possess for it. Once again, each reason here is derived from Scripture.

A third example is the one calling us to bring our needs to Jesus. Why should one do so? Bring your needs to Jesus because no problem is too small for his attention; no problem is too sizeable for his ability and no problem is too stubborn for his authority. As in the second example, this example has three points. Notice, also, that the points have been stated, almost in a poetic format. The purpose of this technique is to help the hearer remember the points. It is a creative way of ensuring members will want to remember the sermon once they have walked away from the service, or from the preaching event. Not only will they want to remember the sermon; they will actually make sure it does not escape their memory.

A fourth example is the one talking about God-given success. The theme is "God-given success is possible." As previously noted, this example leaves the reader hanging. In what way is God-given success possible? God-given success is possible when we live for God, when we look for God and when we learn from God. As with the previous example, the points in this example are all derived from Scripture. Therefore, what you now have in all these four examples is a theme and its main points. The main points help to answer the question prompted by the theme, and when clearly stated, the theme and main points specify the purpose of your sermon.

Exercises

Study the following passages of Scripture and develop a theme from each of them. Remember, the theme should be seven words or less.

1. John 3:16

2. 2 Chronicles 7:14

3. Revelation 21:1–4

4. Isaiah 11:1–9

5. Matthew 1:17–21

6. Psalm 23

Chapter 6

The Theme and Main Points

THE SERMON OUTLINE HAS several ingredients: the sermon title, the sermon text, the general purpose, the particular purpose, the theme and main points. The main points come from the sermon text. The main points of the sermon must be true to the text. As the famed philosopher and theologian, Ramesh Richard says, the sermon must always be at the mercy of the text. The text should never be at the mercy of the sermon. Here is where your study of the text pays off. Let me use the examples you have seen already in order to see how this works.

Let me begin with a short passage from 2 Tim 4:6–8, which says: "For I am already being poured out like a drink offering, and the time has come for my departure. I have fought the good fight; I have finished the race; I have kept the faith. Now there is in store for me the crown of righteousness, which the Lord, the righteous judge, will award to me on that day, and not only to me, but also to all who have longed for his appearing."

What I do with this text is to look at the main idea in each verse of the text. The running theme, as I see it, is the fact that the Christian life is a challenging life. That idea seems to run through the three verses. But what about each verse individually? What specific idea dominates verse 6, for example? The idea in verse 6 has to do with death, specifically because the apostle Paul is talking about his departure, which is a figurative description of his death. To be sure, he is talking about the price he is about to pay for his faith in Christ. I look, therefore, for a creative and memorable way to express this idea in a way that applies to every believer in Jesus Christ, without compromising the meaning of the text.

Your task, then, as the preacher, is to link the main point of verse 6 with the theme. Therefore, it will run something like this: The Christian life is a challenging life because we have a price to pay for it. From point number one, I move on to point number two, which will be the content of verse 7. It reads, "I have fought the good fight, I have finished the race, I have kept the faith." This verse talks about the part Paul had to play in ministry. I draw that idea from the verbal structure of the verse. It has three sentences beginning with "I have." Thus, the second point, when linked to the theme and the first point will run something like this: The Christian life is a challenging life because we have a price to pay for it, and because we have a part to play in it.

The third point comes from verse 8, which talks about a crown Paul expects to earn at the end of the age. Once again, I look for a creative way to put that verse in a single point format. As I see it, it talks about the prize to be possessed. Hence, once linked to the theme and the first two points, the theme and main points will run something like this: The Christian life is a challenging life because we have a price to pay for it, because we have a part to play in it, and also because we have a prize to possess from it. What we now have is a sermon outline that gives you, the preacher, an overview of what your sermon will look like once you preach it. Thus, the outline page of this sermon will look like this:

- Title: "The Christian Life"
- Text: 2 Tim 4:6–8
- General Purpose: To inform
- Particular Purpose: To inform the believers at Geneva Methodist Church that the Christian life is a challenging life because we have a price to pay for it, we have a part to play in it and we have a prize to possess from it.

- Theme: The Christian life is a challenging life

  I. Because we have a price to pay for it (6)

  II. Because we have a part to play in it (7)

  III. Because we have a prize to possess from it (8)

Let me draw your attention to two things about the main points. The main points can be numbered using Arabic numerals, Roman numerals or letters such as A, B, C, D, and so on. Just use the numbering or lettering most convenient for you. Second, notice how I attach a specific verse of Scripture to the point that summarizes it. It helps the preacher to connect each point to its relevant text. Next, let me draw from another example whose partial outline we have already considered. This comes from 2 Chronicles 26:3–5, which says: "Uzziah was sixteen years old when he became king, and he reigned in Jerusalem fifty-two years. His mother's name was Jecoliah, and she was from Jerusalem. He did what was right in the eyes of the Lord, just as his father Amaziah had done. He sought God during the days of Zechariah, who instructed him in the fear of God. As long as he sought the Lord, God gave him success."

Upon looking at that passage, the preacher needs to determine what theme runs through those three verses. The first time I saw the passage from a preacher's perspective, what came to mind was the idea of God-given success. That idea seems to be the running theme. Indeed, it seems to be the running theme among the kings of Judah, where a successful king was a person who feared the Lord, and an unsuccessful king was one who disobeyed the Lord. How did he become successful? Seemingly, the first step toward success for him was to do what was right in the eyes of the Lord. In other words, he lived for God. Indeed, living for God seems to be a summary of doing right in the eyes of the Lord. Hence, if I were to link that section of the text to the theme, it would run something like this: God-given success is possible when we live for God. This move puts my first point in place.

Moving on to the next idea in the text, we see another element that gives us the second point, namely, "He sought the Lord in the days of Zechariah." A summary statement for that passage, arguably, would say he looked for God. That statement gives me the content for the second point. Thus, if I were to link the second point with the theme and the first point, it would read as follows: God-given success is possible when we live for God and when we look for God.

I do the same thing with the third point. It says, ". . .who instructed him in the fear of the Lord." Again, a summary statement for that text, arguably, would say he learned from God. As with the first and second point, that statement gives me the content for the third point, and linking the third point with the theme and the first two points, it would run something like this: God-given success is possible when we live for God, when we look for God and when we learn from God. The outline page for the sermon would thus look like this:

- Title: "God-Given Success"
- Text: 2 Chronicles 4:3–5
- General Purpose: To inform
- Particular Purpose: To inform members of Geneva Methodist Church that God-given success is possible when we live for God, when we look for God and when we learn from God.
- Theme: God-given success is possible

  I.   When we live for God (4)

  II. When we look for God (5a)

  III. When we learn from God (5b)

Again, you can number the main points in whichever way you wish, provided it is most convenient for you. One more example should help make this section clearer. I take it from Mark 1:29–34. It says: "As soon as they left the synagogue, they went with James and John to the home of Simon and Andrew. Simon's mother-in-law was in bed with a fever, and they told Jesus about her. Jesus went to her, took her hand and helped her up. The fever left her, and she began to wait on them. That evening, after sunset, the people brought all the sick and demon possessed to Jesus. The whole town gathered at the door. Jesus healed many who had various diseases. He also cast out many demons. He would not let the demons speak because they knew who he was."

A deeper look at that passage reveals one theme running through the passage. As I see it, the theme is something in the neighborhood of bringing problems to Jesus. Hence, if I were to make that theme relevant to my audience, it should run something like this: "Bring your problems to Jesus." But why should my hearers bring their problems to Jesus? Verses 29 through 31 seem to give me the first clue, which was Simon's mother-in-law lying in bed with a fever. It does not seem to be a king-size problem. To be sure, it seems quite a small problem compared to someone battling a terminal illness. But they told Jesus about her anyway. Thus, one could say a good reason for bringing one's problem to Jesus is: no problem is too small for his attention.

From there, I move to the second point, and I see the glaring contrast between having one case of a fever and many, many cases of various diseases, including demon possession. That is surely a king-size problem. But they brought those problems to Jesus, and Jesus tackled them with ease. Hence, another reason why you should bring your problems to Jesus is because no problem is too sizeable for his ability. Thus, if I were to link this point with the theme and first point, it should run something like this: bring your problems to Jesus because no problem is too small for his attention and no problem is too sizeable for his ability.

A third point comes from the fact that the demons kept wanting to speak, but Jesus would not let them speak. That means the problem was a stubborn one. Thus, a third reason why one should bring one's problems to Jesus is because no problem is too stubborn for his authority. Once again, if I were to link this point with the theme and the first two points, it should run something like this: bring your problems to Jesus because no problem is too small for his attention, no problem is too sizeable for his ability, and no problem is too stubborn for his authority. This result then helps to create the following contents for the outline page:

- Title: "Bringing Your Problems"
- Text: Mark 1:29–34
- General Purpose: To challenge
- Particular Purpose: To challenge believers in Geneva Methodist Church to bring their problems to Jesus because no problem is too small for his attention, no problem is too sizeable for his ability, and no problem is too stubborn for his authority.
- Theme: Bring your problems to Jesus

I. No problem is too small for his attention (26–31)

II. No problem is too sizeable for his ability (32–34a)

III. No problem is too stubborn for his authority (34b)

I have attached the verses summarized by each point to the points themselves. I now move to a long text, which I will not describe as I did with the previous examples. It is John 11:17–44. Here is how the outline page would look like:

- Title: "Jesus Feels Your Pain"
- Text: John 11:17–44
- General Purpose: To assure
- Particular Purpose: to assure members of Geneva Methodist Church that Jesus feels their pain.
- Theme: Jesus feels your pain

I. Because he comes to you (17–20)

II. Because he comforts you (21–27)

III. Because he calls you (28–31)

IV. Because he cries with you (32–35)

V. Because he cares for you (36–40)

VI. Because he cures you (41–44)

The first point takes note of the fact that Jesus went to the home of Martha and Mary. The second point notes that Jesus comforts them with some powerful and reassuring words. The third point observes that Jesus asked for Mary. The fourth point notes that Jesus cried with Martha, Mary, and the Jews. The fifth point focuses on how Jesus demonstrated his care for Lazarus by being deeply moved. The sixth point shows how Jesus cured Lazarus by raising him from the dead.

The final item to appear on the outline is the conclusion. The conclusion of the sermon is just as important as the other segments of the sermon. No part of the sermon is more important than the other specifically because the whole sermon is the part of the whole counsel of God's word. I will say more about it in a separate section. For now, let us move on to the introduction of the sermon.

Exercises

Study the following passages of Scripture and construct sermon outlines from them.

1. John 3:16

2. 2 Chronicles 7:14

3. Revelation 21:1–4

4. Isaiah 11:1–9

5. Matthew 1:17–21

6. Psalm 23

Chapter 7

The Introduction of the Sermon

ONE OF THE MOST important favors you could do for yourself, as a preacher, is to write your sermon out in full. A problem once stated is half-solved, says Dale Carnegie. This includes writing down the introduction. But what should one say in the introduction and how should one present it? A bad introduction prepares the audience for a painful sermonic experience. A good introduction creates anticipation. Let me, here, specify what a good introduction would look like.

First, a good introduction gets the attention of the people. A good introduction is arresting. It makes your audience want to be there rather than anywhere else at that time. It gives your audience the impression you have a message for them from God. It makes the audience have a sense of anticipation that something very important is about to be said, something life-defining and eternally transformative. One will not always hit a home run with an introduction. But one should aspire toward stating an attention-grabbing introduction.

One way to give a good introduction is to begin with a story that ties into both the sermon title and the sermon theme. The story could be a true-to-life story, or merely a story relaying events that need not have happened. In either case, you, the preacher must be sure to convey this fact. If it is not a true story, acknowledge it. If it is a true story, acknowledge this fact. Either way, a good story that ties into the message well is always a good way to begin. Stories relevant to the message will always get people's attention.

Another way to give a good introduction is to begin the sermon by restating a catchy phrase or a catchy statement that someone else, besides you, stated. The person could be a well-known figure or an obscure person, in which case you, the preacher, will have to let your audience know. That phrase or statement should ideally be related to the topic you are trying to address, directly or indirectly. For example, suppose your sermon is about fear. You could start your sermon as follows: "A well-known American leader famously said, 'The only thing to fear is fear itself.'" You could then build on that idea as you lead your audience through the introduction of your sermon.

Whereas catchy phrases are often not as effective as stories, if stated correctly, they become powerful tools for getting your audience's attention and for putting your points across. They help to get the attention of the audience. However, even though they are good for getting attention, their effects wear out as the sermon progresses. Once you use those phrases, you must work hard to maintain the momentum already gained and keep them listening to you. Hence, the challenge you face, as the preacher, is to keep them attentive throughout the sermonic process.

Second, a good introduction creates a need. More specifically, a good introduction creates a need in the hearts and minds of the audience to listen to you. You, the preacher, must ask yourself the following question: how can I position the introduction in a way that gives the audience a reason to listen to what I have to say? At this point, the purpose of your sermon comes in handy. If it is to challenge your audience, you must ask yourself what sorts of challenging expressions or statements you can use to get the audience interested.

Consider the topic generated earlier from 2 Chronicles 26:3–5, namely, the topic of God-given success. One way to create the need among your audience is to ask the question, "Do you want to be successful in God's eyes? Have you always desired to be successful in a certain field in a way that meets God's approval? If you do, may I point you to a portion of Scripture that gives you a blue-print for success in God's eyes? Have you ever felt as if you were a failure before God's eyes? Did you do anything to overcome that thinking? Would you like to know what you need to do to be successful in God's eyes?"

Notice what this kind of introduction does. It speaks to the need, among your audience, of wanting to succeed. Most people want to succeed in life. Very few like to fail. This kind of introduction helps to keep the audience glued to the kinds of things you could say based on the text. It helps your audience to stay alert. Do not be surprised if some of them whip out their pens and pieces of paper to write down what they can from your presentation. This is because you are addressing a felt need, the sermon itself is biblically based, and it comes from your time of prayer in your prayer closet.

Let us try another example, taken from the Gospel of Mark 1:29–34. The title of that sermon is "Bringing Problems to Jesus." In your introduction for a sermon of this kind, you can create a need by asking true-to-life questions or making true-to-life statements such as: I am sure you have problems. They could be health problems, financial problems, problems at work or problems at home. How do you solve those problems? Have you succeeded in solving them? Let me point you to someone who wants you to bring your problems to him. His name is Jesus." It need not be this brief. You will need to say more here, including talking about your own problems and how God helped you through them.

Once again, an introduction of this kind creates a need. It gives a reason for the audience to sit there and listen to you. It is also consistent with the purpose of your sermon. It helps you to address an issue or a concern members of the congregation may likely have. Sermons of this kind will almost always speak to someone because problem-free individuals are rare to find. Just about everyone in life has a problem that needs to be addressed.

Just to drive the point home, I add another example from the story of the death of Lazarus. Basing the sermon on John

11:17–44, the theme I find prevailing throughout those verses is the claim that Jesus felt the pain of the bereaved, namely, Mary, Martha, and the Jews who came to mourn with them. In a sermon I preached on this very text, my theme and main points were as follows: Jesus feels your pain because he comes to you, he comforts you, he calls you, he cries with you, he cares for you, and he cures you. The introduction of the sermon will, therefore, create a need by highlighting how Jesus feels the pain of his people.

Therefore, I would introduce the sermon as follows: "Have you ever gone through moments of intense emotional or physical pain and wondered if you were the only one walking through that pain? Do you ever wonder if someone else feels your pain? Walking alone during times of pain and suffering can be a very lonely road. Quite possibly, you are walking through that pain right now. Allow me to point you to someone who knows your pain, possibly much better than you do. This person weeps with you during your times of trial and suffering."

An introduction positioned in this way will certainly get the attention of the suffering individual. It piques the person's interest, leading him or her to wait for the answer to the questions raised at the introductory remarks. The audience in pain will want to know who their co-sufferer is, and what evidence one has for believing that at least one person exists who feels their pain. Positioned in this way, the preacher will get the attention of his audience throughout the introduction.

A good introduction not only gets attention or creates a need. A good introduction also gives an overview of the sermon by revealing the theme and main points before transitioning to the main sermon body. Ordinarily, this is called the proposition of the sermon. When you give your audience the proposition of the sermon, namely, the theme and main points, your audience gets an idea of the general direction of your sermon, and it helps them walk with you through the sermonic process. This move is advantageous for you and for your audience.

First, the audience will not be lost, wondering what you might be trying to convey. They will be with you almost every step of the way in your sermonic process. They will know what point you will be explaining, illustrating and applying. They will know exactly where you will be once you begin your transition from one point to another. This process does the congregation a favor because you will not only be empowering them spiritually, you will be giving them a reason to want to listen to you even more in the coming days should you have another opportunity to speak again.

Second, you are more likely to stay focused on the topic without wandering off in tangents. Many preachers have made the mistake of wanting to say everything they know in one sermon rather than knowing what to say in that sermon. When preachers try to say everything they know, they almost inevitably lose their audience. A multi-topic sermon is likely to leave your audience confused. However, a sermon with a theme and main points will, more likely than not, keep your audience attentive throughout your sermonic process.

Third, your audience will remember most of what you say. I use this method of preaching every Sunday. Members of my congregation are always able to give a fairly accurate summary of what the sermon of the day was, including the illustrations used and the applications made. In other words, a great opportunity for discipleship arises from using this method. When you preach a series of sermons on any book of the Bible using this method, it helps members of the congregation develop outlines that summarize the books of the Bible in a fairly memorable way.

Fourth, a good introduction highlights the context of the sermon text. The introduction shows how that passage of Scripture fits into the entire chapter to which it belongs and, in some cases, the entire book of the Bible, especially if it is a one-chapter book such as Obadiah, Philemon, 2 John, 3 John and Jude. Such an introduction needs to mention something about the theme or topic before the passage to be exposited. Text without context is pretext, the Bible scholars tell us. Preaching without paying attention to context will likely result in misinterpretations of Scripture. The preacher must always preach with a keen eye to the context of the text.

The ingredients of the introduction, include getting the attention of the audience, creating a need in the hearts and minds of the listeners, drawing attention to the context of the preached text, and presenting an overview of the sermon with a proposition. The introduction will then transition into the main body of the sermon. Once the transition into the text is made, the audience will be adequately set for a dose of great preaching for the next twenty minutes or more. How exactly this is accomplished will be demonstrated later. The next section will focus on what to do with the main points. For now, we sufficiently say the ingredients I mention above will help you, the preacher, position your sermon quite effectively if adequately used.

Exercises

Select one or more of the passages of Scripture below and develop a sermon introduction from that passage. You have already worked on these passages before.

1. John 3:16

2. 2 Chronicles 7:14

3. Revelation 21:1–4

4. Isaiah 11:1–9

5. Matthew 1:17–21

6. Psalm 23

Chapter 8

The Explanation of the Main Points

HOW MANY POINTS SHOULD a sermon have? No particular rule
exists specifying how many points a sermon should have. As Jef-
frey Frymire, former professor of preaching at Asbury Seminary,
wisely says, a good sermon must have at least one point! If no point
exists for any given sermon, then it is just that—pointless! A pointless sermon leaves the audience wondering why the speaker is on
the pulpit saying nothing and expecting members of the audience
to repeat it! What the preacher will be trying to convey will remain
unclear for the duration of the sermon. That fact explains why
people walk away from a church service scratching their heads
asking, "What was that about?!" A rule of thumb is that any sermon must have at least one point.

Frymire also notes how the text determines the structure of
the sermon. Avoid forcing points into the text that do not appear
in that text. When you force meaning into the text, you are forcing
the text to say what is not there. At that point, the text is at the
mercy of the sermon. In this section, if you are joining the preaching ministry without some roadmap for preaching, rejoice! You
will, hopefully, get some guidance and direction here.

Once you have developed an outline of your sermon and
have written out your introduction in full, your next task is to take
your audience into the text of Scripture. The assumption in the

method I am proposing is that each point will be a summary of the text of Scripture. Hence, an exposition of the text of Scripture highlights the summarized points to be made. Always connect the point to the text and the text to the point by showing how the point is an interpretation of the text. This helps the listener understand the text and it also helps the listener remain alert throughout the sermonic process.

Hence, the first stage of developing your point is the explanation stage. At this point, the preacher does what theologians call "exegesis." Exegesis is the task of explaining the meaning of the text in question. At this stage, the preacher will engage in a systematic explanation of each word in the text of Scripture covered by the point in question. Your explanation, as the preacher, ought to be simple and clear. Your explanation, also, needs to be accessible and repeatable by the person listening to you. Ensure you explain words, phrases and sentences by putting them in your own words. When you do this, you are allowing God to use your personality as a conduit of divine truth through the explanation of the written word.

One of the key helpers of your explanation, as noted at the very beginning of this book, is the use of Bible commentaries, study Bibles, concordances and, if you are well-versed in Greek and Hebrew, the use of the original languages. Of course, I understand not every preacher has the time or the money to go to seminary to learn Greek or Hebrew. That fact seems to be the case with most of us. Your best recourse, then, is to use *Strong's Concordance* with Greek and Hebrew Lexicon, which is readily available online. You will find it very helpful in helping you find the meaning of the studied word in its original language.

Bible commentaries are also helpful. But the authors of those commentaries ought to be scholars committed to the authority of Scripture. When choosing to use Bible commentaries, bear that fact in mind. This piece of advice comes to you because some Bible commentators may not necessarily agree with you about some key doctrines of the Bible. In such cases, seek the guidance and counsel of your pastors, assuming they too remain committed to the authority of the word of God. If they are, they will most likely know which commentaries to use and which ones to avoid.

As noted earlier, another helpful tool is a study Bible. The downside to a study Bible is the fact that it does not really give you a verse-by-verse explanation of every text of scripture. In such cases, you will have to go back to the use of commentaries. However, if all you have is a study Bible, it is a great resource to have, and will be of great value in helping you explain given passages of Scripture

What you must avoid, while explaining the text, is the attempt to be sophisticated. Sophistication only complicates the message and denies your audience the opportunity to receive the word God has placed in your hands. The kind of sophistication I have in mind here is the attempt to give your audience the meaning of each word in the original language of Scripture, namely, Greek or Hebrew. The moment a preacher mentions the Greek word in Greek or the Hebrew word in Hebrew, the preacher loses a portion of the audience. I liken the idea of using the original language in preaching to "taking the food back to the cooking stove." Hebrew and Greek are meant only for the preparation stage and not for the proclamation stage, unless, of course, you are preaching to a Hebrew or Greek audience!

Preparing your sermon is similar to cooking food, as some Bible scholar said in the past. When you cook your food, you ensure it is ready by the time you bring it to the table for people to eat. Similarly, when you prepare your sermon and look at the meaning of the text in the original language, you are preparing spiritual food for the audience. Once you have all the meanings of the relevant words adequately explained, you do not need to return to the original language to decipher further meanings from the text. It would be analogous to the chef taking your plate of food back to the cooking stove to cook it further.

For that reason, the use of the original languages should be confined only to the preparation stage. The use of the original language is for the preacher to enhance a more meaningful explanation of the text in the language of the people. Do your best to leave all allusions to the original language at the preparation stage on your desk. Referring to the original languages of the Bible is absolutely important for explaining the meaning of the text. If you, the preacher, do not know the original language, a concordance will help you determine the word and its meaning in the original text. But you must avoid the temptation to bring the original language and its use to the pulpit. The pulpit is meant for the proclamation of the word of God in the most accessible way possible by using the language known best by your audience.

I had a friend who always found it necessary to use either Greek or Hebrew words on the pulpit as he was preaching. He believed it was evidence he had done his work of preparing the biblical text. In a certain real sense, he was right. However, he had a major problem. Every time he used those Greek words or Hebrew words, he lost his audience. The audience did not care one bit how much Hebrew or Greek he knew. They just wanted to hear the word of God. Besides, this friend could not even pronounce those Greek and Hebrew words fluently. He stumbled over his pronunciations so obviously that even his audience, who did not understand that language, knew he messed up. It became such a huge distraction to the general flow of his sermons. Taken by themselves, however, the sermons were really good. It is his overuse of the Greek and Hebrew words that diluted the power of his sermon.

The important thing to remember, here, is each point needs to be explained clearly and in a way your readers will find understandable and accessible. Their understanding of the preached word should be clear enough to be repeated by your audience, in their own words, to individuals who missed your preaching assignment. You as the preacher must strive for clarity of expression, pacing yourself in ways that allow your audience to take copious notes as they listen to you.

Always strive for clarity in your presentation of the biblical material. It is a responsibility God has placed upon your shoulders and he is cheering you on as you work through the text, explaining it to his people. Recall my earlier illustration of how I come up with a sermon outline each day as I go into my prayer closet.

During that moment of prayer, I seek God's guidance and direction for a word he will allow me to give his people someday. That dynamic plays itself out every day I walk into my prayer closet. My suspicion is that you too will sense that dynamic as you maintain a powerful prayer vigil and life. During those moments, God speaks either indirectly through his word, or through a deep and strong impression in your being about what he wants you to say. I have had this feeling numerous times. Whenever I respond in obedience to God, I see the results at once, and God reminds me of his faithfulness by that very response.

Therefore, each point should have an explanation—an exposition of what the text relating to it is about. Each point should be made clear by the use of language your audience will understand. Avoid sophistication that fails to achieve the intended goals of the sermon. Moreover, each point needs to be connected to the passage of Scripture, and the preacher must always strive to tie the portion of Scripture to that point. That fact should always remain clear. The explanation of a given text of Scripture is the proclamation of God's word at its finest. Your task, then, is to remain available, always, for just such an opening and outpouring of God's message to you.

Exercise

The exercise in the previous section asked you to develop an introduction for a passage of your choice, which you selected from a list given to you. From that very text, whose outline you also developed, explain each portion of Scripture represented by the points you developed from that text.

Chapter 9

The Illustration of the Main Points

PREACHING IS FUN! IT should be. You are right at the center of God's will when you stand before his people expounding the gospel message. But it is also serious business. You have to approach it with fear and trembling. Your sermons can do one of three things: draw your audience closer to God, pull them further away from God if they are not alert, or leave them spiritually stagnant. This fact is staggering. If you stick to Scripture, you have an excellent chance of drawing them closer to God. If you walk away from Scripture in your preaching, you risk misleading them or leaving them stagnant, assuming they are not alert.

One of the fun parts of preaching is expounding Scripture through the joy of illustrating the text with relevant examples. Here is where members of your audience see how you approach that text based on your quiet time with God during the preparation stage. It makes the preaching event enjoyable both for you and for your audience. It keeps your audience alert, listening to every word you proclaim from the pulpit. Every time I introduce a story to illustrate a portion of the text, I can tell from the facial expressions of my audience how their level of interest grows. They are quite familiar with the method I am describing here, and so they know exactly when the illustration is about to come at just about every stage of the preaching.

Some wonder whether the use of illustrations is biblical. Should one incorporate present-day events into the text of Scripture? Would that not amount to adulterating the purity of the text with non-biblical events? Incorporating present-day or contemporary events into the text of Scripture is a practice as old as the Bible itself. We find examples of this truth in both the Old and the New Testament. Both the major prophets and the minor prophets used illustrations to convey spiritual truth. Consider, for example, how a book as brief as Obadiah uses illustrations when he asks: "If thieves came to you, if robbers in the night—O what a disaster awaits you—would they not steal only as much as they wanted? If grape-pickers came to you, would they not leave a few grapes?" Isaiah the prophet used illustrations to convey his message. Both Jeremiah and Ezekiel used illustrations to convey their message. Many minor prophets did the same.

In the New Testament, the teachings of Jesus are filled with illustrations. All the parables of Jesus were illustrations of a teaching he was conveying to his hearers. He masterfully incorporated parables and stories into his teaching, stories we consider timeless. The apostles incorporated illustrations in their teachings. We find that in the writings of Paul, Peter and James. Without question, therefore, the use of illustrations to convey biblical truths is a practice we find throughout Scripture. Hence, using illustrations in your sermon is biblical.

Using them is not only biblical, but also necessary, giving your sermon an attention-grabbing value. They draw your audience into the event of explaining the text with greater clarity. They keep your audience focused on the point you are trying to convey. They make your sermon memorable because you present the sermon in an engaging manner. They keep your audience interested in hearing what the final push of your sermon will look like. A sermon without illustrations runs the risk of being dull and boring. That is why Jesus used them throughout his ministry. They appeal to the creative part of our human brains to keep us interested and focused on the topic of the text being presented to us.

The good news about illustrations is their availability. In the past people depended on their memories of relevant stories to gather illustrations for specific sermons. All they needed to do was to engage their minds, recall the stories and use them for the specific texts. This way of retrieving illustrations continues to this day. I have done it many times, and I continue to do it. Thus, memory could be a readily available source of illustrations for a given sermon.

A second source of illustrations is an illustration book written for the purpose of storing specific illustrations for preaching. Usually, the authors of the illustration books catalogue those illustrations into specific topics for quick and easy references. I have used and continue to use Michael Green's *Illustrations for Biblical Preaching* as a reliable source of illustrations, as well as *The Complete Speaker's Source Book* by Eleanor Doan. Such sources are good in that they remain helpful for the preacher struggling to find illustrations for a specific point in the sermon. Of course, they do have their limitations. One limitation involves the fact that they contain illustrations that would have been useful if they did not make reference to outdated materials such as cassettes or rotary phones. Still, one could adapt them by using contemporary analogies.

A third source of illustrations could be the day-to-day stories published in both the electronic media, the print media and, sometimes, the social media. I have found relevant stories from these sources powerfully illustrating the biblical text in ways that enhance the recollection of the sermons preached. One could easily collect such stories and save them in a repository of illustrations for future use. Whenever I see a story I find meaningful and powerful, I save it in my device. I need not have a sermon ready for the use of that story. Just the same, since I do not know when I could use the story in the future, I simply save it. That practice allows me to return to the story when I need to use it to illustrate one of the points of my sermons.

A fourth source of illustrations could be personal events and testimonies in your life as a preacher. Telling such stories can be sources of inspiration to your hearers, especially coming from the fact that you are a living witness of the event you are describing. But as you relay the story to your audience, guard against drawing attention to yourself at the expense of keeping your audience focused on God. In any preaching event, God, and God alone, takes the center stage. If your story or testimony keeps God at the center, then you need not worry about telling it.

Visual aids are a powerful fifth source of illustrations. Visual aids bring certain truths of Scripture to life. The preacher using visual aids must, of course, remember to bring the relevant paraphernalia to the pulpit. Otherwise, the whole presentation will break down. I have used skits, musical presentations and drama to illustrate specific biblical texts. These provide powerful visual aids for the listener. Care must be taken in the use of visual aids to ensure they do not draw the people away from the original message of Scripture.

Another important source of illustrations is the biblical text itself. One could quite conceivably use a Bible story to illustrate the text being expounded. However, since the Bible is the text we are trying to explain, the preacher needs to make it clear in the sermon that the Bible story in question is being used to illustrate a spiritual truth. In James 4:11 and 17, the apostle James used the story of Job and Elijah to illustrate the point he was conveying to his readers. Also, the apostle Peter used the story of Sodom and Gomorrah in 2 Peter 2:6 to illustrate the idea that God punishes sin and saves godly people from trials.

Several areas of caution need to be identified in the use of illustrations. First, illustrations are not meant to entertain the audience, though some of them do have an entertainment value. Their purpose is to enhance the teaching of the biblical text. One must ensure their use is primarily to clarify the message of Scripture. However, if illustrations come with an entertaining value or an enjoyment value, then that aspect becomes a double bonus for the preaching event. Precisely because of these additional values that members of the congregation will remember how they were used.

Enjoying a sermon in the church is not wrong at all. But enjoyment is not the ultimate goal of the sermon.

Second, illustrations should not be used as a source of religious authority, except, of course, a Bible story used as an illustration. The text of Scripture is the source of religious authority. Using wise sayings, for example, as the source of authority in a preaching event misleads the congregation into thinking that the wise saying comes from Scripture. Some statements such as "God helps those who help themselves" may sound quite wise, for example, but sayings of this kind are not in Scripture and should not be used as a message of the Bible. The point I am pressing here is simple: illustrations are a means to an end. They are not an end in themselves.

Third, illustrations should not obscure the message of the text. The preacher must be careful not to give illustrations more weight than Scripture. Illustrations, if misused, can take a train of thought away from Scripture into a destiny not intended by the text being expounded and, indeed, into an idea completely outside the Bible. This fact has played itself out on numerous preaching occasions among preachers who take the preaching event merely for its entertainment value rather than for its edificatory value.

Fourth, use the right illustrations for the right text of Scripture. Erroneously using illustrations misses the point of illustrations and runs the risk of drawing the attention of the audience to the preacher rather than to the text. Moreover, members of the audience will have a hard time connecting the point of the misused illustration to the text of Scripture itself. They will, quite understandably, walk away from the preaching event, again, scratching their heads wondering why the illustration was used in the first place.

Illustrations play an important role in the sermonic process. They help convey the meaning of the text in a creative way. God, through Jesus Christ, has used illustrations to convey his message to his people. He has used prophets to do the same in the past. He can use you in the present to speak to his people. Therefore, begin collecting all the stories you can muster. You never know when you will use them. Your sermon, then, should have the following process: an introduction, followed by explaining the first point, followed by illustrating the first point.

Exercise

The exercises in previous sections asked you to develop an introduction for a passage of your choice, and explain each portion of scripture represented by the points you developed from that text, which you selected from a list given to you. In this exercise, develop your point further by finding a relevant illustration from any of the sources mentioned in this chapter, and add it creatively onto that explanation.

Chapter 10

The Application of the Main Points

YOU HAVE EXPLAINED THE text in your first (or only) point, by putting in your own words what the text means to you. You have also illustrated that point using specific examples to enhance your explanation. Your next step is to apply the text by allowing that text to speak to the audience in a way that will make a lasting impact in their lives. What sort of move does the task of application involve or entail? Applying the text, or putting it into practice, begins by asking the question, "How does this text work for me?" Or "How does this text work for our situation?" Applying the text is biblical. The apostle James famously said, "Do not merely listen to the word, and so deceive yourselves. Do what it says" (Jas 1:22). This is a command. Therefore, reading the text or hearing the spoken word of God without applying it in one's life seems to border on disobedience.

The application part is an important stage of the preaching process. It is where the sermon comes alive in one's life. At this stage, the preacher uses the word of God to challenge or help bring about some kind of change from the audience. At this stage, the preacher issues a call to action. The preacher challenges the hearer of the word to live consistently with the requirements of that word. The preacher may even be forced, with divine authority, to "command" the audience gently to follow a prescribed course of action.

It is where the word of God brings about the desired transformation in the life of the hearer of the spoken word.

The task of the preacher, at the application stage, is to tie the word of God to the life of the hearer. The preacher does so by identifying areas in the life of the audience where Scripture speaks directly to them. It might be a command that must be obeyed, a promise that could be claimed, a sin that needs to be avoided or a burden that needs to be surrendered. Hence, challenging the believer is not the only task of the application. Some texts of Scripture, when properly applied, encourage the listeners by bringing comfort, usually to the bereaved or to individuals who suffer some kinds of loss. Other texts assure believers to entrust their lives to God more and more in the midst of pain and suffering. The preacher will help tie these areas of their lives to the text of Scripture under consideration.

Let me cite a few examples from a few of the outlines I used earlier. I will take liberty to adjust some of the outlines for purposes of demonstration. Beginning with the passage from 2 Chronicles 26:3–5, we have the following outline:

- Title: "God-Given Success"

- Text: 2 Chronicles 4:3–5

- General Purpose: To inform

- Particular Purpose: To inform members of Geneva Methodist Church that God-given success comes when we live for God, when we look for God and when we learn from God

- Theme: God-given success comes

    I. When we live for God

    II. When we look for God

    III.When we learn from God

Let's take the first point. How can we apply it? To do this, we need to go to the scriptural text from which it is derived. It runs as follows, in reference to Uzziah: "He did what was right in the eyes of the Lord." Assuming you have already illustrated the text, the application could run as follows: "If you want to be successful, you have to do what is right in the eyes of the Lord. Your friends may prescribe what they think, in their own eyes, is right for you to do. But you must ask yourself, is this right in the eyes of the Lord? When you break the speed limit on the road just because everyone else is doing it, is this right in the eyes of the Lord? When I speak falsely about my brother or sister in the congregation, that is not right in the eyes of the Lord, even if everyone else could be doing it. If you want to be successful in the eyes of the Lord, you must always ask yourself whether what you are about to do is something God will approve of." The application tries to tie specific texts of Scripture to the listener's life.

Let us now take the second point. It says God-given success comes when we look for God. The passage of Scripture that helped me make that point, speaking of King Uzziah, says: "He sought the Lord in the days of Zechariah." How, then, does one look for God? The application of this point or, for that matter, this text, runs something similar to this: "If you want to be successful, always look for God. Seek his face in prayer. Seek his face by reading his word. Seek his face by fellowshipping with other believers. Seek the Lord by worshiping in church every Sunday, or whenever you get the opportunity. A recipe for success in God's eyes involves seeking God. Do you want to be successful in God's eyes? Then look for God." As with the first point, the attempt to tie this text of Scripture to the listener's life is necessary for an effective application.

Let us look at the last point. It says God-given success comes when we learn from God. Once again, the passage of Scripture that helped me make that point, speaking of King Uzziah, says: ". . .who instructed him in the fear of the Lord." How does one apply this passage? The application would run something like this: "If you want to be successful, you need to learn from God. One of the most obvious ways to learn from God is by reading the word of God, studying the word of God and memorizing the word of God. So, learn from God by studying his word. Learn from God not only by studying his word; but learn from God, also, by listening to his word. Hearing a preached sermon would be a good starting point. Joining a Bible study would be a good starting point. If you want to be successful, learning from God is a key ingredient."

The sermon itself will lead your congregation toward a conclusion that will, in a certain sense, demand a response. The response will be something similar to making a commitment to seek God-given success in life. The conclusion will ask those pointed questions, and I will demonstrate how those questions can be raised.

Let me try another demonstration with a different text of Scripture, one you have seen before if you have read the earlier chapters of this book. It is taken from Mark 1:29–34. These are the initial ingredients of the outline:

- Title: "Bringing Your Problems"

- Text: Mark 1:29–34

- General Purpose: To challenge

- Particular Purpose: To challenge believers in Geneva Methodist Church to bring their problems to Jesus

- Theme: Bring your problems to Jesus

  I. No problem is too small for him

  II. No problem is too sizeable for him

  III.No problem is too stubborn for him

How do we go about applying the first point, namely, "No problem is too small for him"? One way to do this is to ask questions your audience will relate with, such as these: "Do you feel as if your problem is too small for you to bring it even to Jesus simply because you think you will be bothering him? I assure you, no problem is too small for his attention. It might be a problem as simple as that of finding your misplaced keys or your misplaced wallet. It's okay to bring that problem to Jesus. It might be as simple a problem as changing the light bulb in your house. It's okay to bring that problem to Jesus. It might be as simple a problem as having the desire to clean your house. It's okay to ask Jesus to give you the strength to do it or to create that desire in you. Why do you need to bring this problem to Jesus? The answer is simple: no problem is too small for his attention."

Let's try applying the second point, namely, "No problem is too sizeable for him." This is easily relatable. Once again, you, the preacher, can ask your audience a question analogous to the ones you asked at point number one: "Do you feel as if your problem is beyond the power of Jesus to solve? Is it a sickness you are dealing with? Is it a financial difficulty you are dealing with? Have you lost your job? Are you struggling with your marriage? Let me encourage you to bring that problem to Jesus. I acknowledge that the problem is big. I acknowledge that not even I can solve your problem because it is big. But I can point you to someone who can solve that problem for you. His name is Jesus. Bring that problem to Jesus because no problem is too sizable for his ability."

Let us now attempt applying the third point, namely, "No problem is too stubborn for his authority." We proceed, as before, by asking analogous questions. What problem has been nagging you for days, for weeks, for months or even for years? What problem has been troubling you almost consistently and without fail? Bring that problem to Jesus. It does not matter how stubborn that problem is. Bring it to Jesus because it will have to bow to the authority of Jesus. No problem is too stubborn for his authority."

As you can see, the purpose of the application is to bring your hearer from the theoretical stage to the practical stage. The application answers the "So what?" question created by your sermon. As your audience begins to listen to your sermon, they will begin asking themselves, "How do I respond to this sermon?" "What do I need to do in response to what the preacher is saying?" "How can I bring my problem to Jesus"? Once they begin asking those kinds of questions, you are already creating an opportunity for an altar call—a call to action. You are already creating an opportunity for the people to respond to what you have just brought to their understanding, and doing so will be the purpose of the conclusion.

Assuming you have more than one point in your sermon outline, you will need to use transitional sentences between points.

Suppose your connection between the theme and main points is the word "because." The structure of your transition will begin with the theme, followed by the phrase "not only. . . but also. . ." In order to see this structure more clearly, take the following illustration of one of the examples you have seen before. God-given success comes, *not only* by living for God, *but also* by looking for God. This illustration demonstrates the transition between the first point and the second point. Suppose you want to transition between the second point and the third point, your transition could be as follows: God-given success comes, not *only* by living for God, *or* by looking for God, *but also* by learning from God. An illustration of Mark 1:29–34 should help clarify further the use of transitions between all three points, as follows: Bring your problems to Jesus *not only* because no problem is too small for his attention, *or* because no problem is too sizeable for his ability, *but also* because no problem is too stubborn for his authority.

Exercise

The exercises in previous sections asked you to develop an introduction for a passage of your choice, and explain each portion of scripture represented by the points you developed from that text, which you selected from a list given to you. They also asked you to develop your point further by finding a relevant illustration from any of the sources mentioned in this chapter, and add it creatively onto that explanation. Develop the point you have explained and illustrated by applying it to possible members of your audience and, thereafter, do the same with additional points you might have developed, namely, explaining them, illustrating them and applying them.

Chapter 11

The Conclusion of Your Sermon

HERE, THEN, IS THE sermonic process I propose: introduction of the sermon, transition into the theme and main points, explanation of each point, illustration of each point, application of each point, and conclusion of the sermon. As you transition from one point to another, ensure it is a smooth transition without glitches. Once you have completed your transitions between points, you can then explain the new point, illustrate it and apply it. From there, you transition to the conclusion.

The task of the conclusion is to give a final push for the sermon. In it, the preacher makes the final case for what needs to be said. In many ways, the conclusion is the climax of the sermon. It is the point where the preacher is trying to get the audience to reach. It is the sermon's destiny. That is where the preacher challenges the listener to respond. The conclusion has two important ingredients: a recapitulation of the main points and a call to respond to the message in some way.

As a recapitulation of the main points, the conclusion helps the audience to remember what the preacher has been trying to convey throughout the sermon. The preacher helps the audience to remember all the points of the sermon so they will have no excuse for missing the main gist of the sermon. As the preacher of the day, you will need to be both deliberate and intentional at getting your audience to walk with you through this process. Ensure that they really do get the points you are trying to convey. You do not need to overstress the point. You simply need to recollect them. This is because, when you do this effectively, most of them will whip out their pens and pieces of paper, and they will be writing down your points as you speak.

The call to respond, however, takes a slightly different tone. You are, at this point, getting your audience to take the action you were hoping to fulfill. As already noted, it is an invitation for your audience to respond. A popular way of asking your audience to respond is to ask them to raise their hands if they need divine help in fulfilling the goals your sermon was trying to get them toward. Another way of doing this is to get the audience to stand for prayer. This is usually challenging because asking your audience to stand for prayer stretches your audience beyond their comfort zone. Be prepared for a no-response outcome. When you get no response, that is absolutely okay. They may not respond at the precise moment you are issuing the call. However, they may give you a call, or even send you a text message. You just never know, sometimes, what God is accomplishing in the lives of your audience until you hear much later what the Lord has done in their lives.

What you must be careful to do is to ensure you do not manipulate God's people with your altar call. When you begin manipulating people, they will know it. How do you draw the line between issuing a genuine altar call and manipulating your audience? If you ask them to do what the Scripture text does not warrant you to do in that sermon, you will be bordering on manipulating your audience. If you promise more than the Scripture delivers, you will be in danger of manipulating your audience. Your best bet is to stay within the confines of Scripture. Stay away from wrestling the arm of God to do something he has not promised to do. Simply issue the invitation and leave the results to God.

Here is an example of what an altar call would look like, based on the text from 2 Chronicles 26:3–5: "Quite possibly, you want to live a successful life before God. As you take stock of your previous life, you feel as if you could use some help to succeed in the eyes of God. No one else, more than God, wants you to succeed in this endeavor. No one else, more than God, wants you to be successful in life. The surest way I know of to get you on that path to success is to ask God for help through a collective prayer I would like for us to offer to God on your behalf. If you want us to ask God to give you the power to live for him, we are more than ready to do so. If you want us to ask God to give you the power to look for him through the study of his word, we are more than delighted to help you do so. If you want us to ask God to give you the power to learn from him, we will be honored to help you in that regard. If you are here and you desire this kind of success before the eyes of God, please raise your hand so we can pray with you right now."

Let me illustrate, also, how the text from Mark 1:26–34 can help you issue an altar call in the area of bringing your problems to Jesus. You can begin by asking: "What problems do you have today? Have you considered bringing those problems to Jesus? Do you feel your problem is too small for his attention? I want to assure you that he is just as interested in solving that problem as you are, perhaps even more than you are interested in solving it. Let me encourage you to begin asking the Lord to handle that problem you think is too small for him. Do you feel your problem is too sizeable for his ability? I want to assure you that God is able to lift that burden off your shoulders. Just because that burden is too heavy for you to carry does not mean it is too heavy for Jesus to carry. Let me encourage you to begin asking the Lord to handle that problem you think is too small for him. He is more than able and more than willing to carry it for you. Perhaps you are dealing with a stubborn problem. It could be an illness. It could be an addiction of some kind. It could be a problem even with your car, or a stubborn problem with your finances. Bring that problem to Jesus because no problem is too stubborn for his authority. Irrespective of what problem you have, I encourage you to let Jesus carry the burden you are carrying. Do not carry a burden Jesus has promised to carry for you. If you are carrying any burden right now, and you want Jesus to help you out of this burden, would you please raise your hand so I can pray with you a final, concluding prayer?"

As you can see, a text like Mark 1:26–34, when properly outlined, gives you a very handy way of positioning the conclusion for the people. Moreover, you can be sure that as you are presenting the altar call to the congregation, you have the full back-up of the Holy Spirit to bring deep conviction into the lives of those listening to you. Bear in mind, though, that this back-up is on the assumption you have remained in prayer consistently for the ministry God has placed in your hands. Without this consistent prayer, you will simply be going through a method sounding fine on the surface, but is certainly dry and empty of the Spirit's power.

Once you have given your altar call, and have prayed for your congregation, your sermonic process is over. You must ensure, however, that you keep your audience wanting for more by observing the time-slot given to you for preaching. You do not want to keep your audience there longer than necessary. That means you must, in a very literal sense, keep your eye on the clock. When members of your congregation begin to look at their watch to check the time, they are sending you a message, namely, "When will you be ending this?" or "Are you about done here?" or "My goodness, we will be here for eternity!" When that happens, you are well on your way to failing to fulfill your purpose. So, keep your conclusion within the confines of time.

Once you have brought your sermon to its conclusion, you can consider your preaching event completed. However, your life as a preacher continues. Your task at this point is to continue with your preparation for the next sermon. That, indeed, is the life of the preacher, though your work as a preacher is not completed when you end your sermon. Your work continues. If your sermon ends with great affirmation from your audience, expect a second invitation. Expect additional calls to preach again. This is because the style of preaching I describe here connects the people with the word of God. Of course, this means you will need to continue with the practice I describe in the second chapter of this work. Every quiet time you have is an opportunity to hear from God, and to formulate a word that speaks to you first before you can take it out to the people. The more you keep this fact in perspective, the likelier you are to have a new sermon for the people of God each time you are invited to speak, and the more you speak a new word fresh from the throne of God, the more you will be invited to speak.

Exercise

On the introduction and the main points you have been writing, add the conclusion to complete your written sermon. Be sure to summarize the main points and give the final push to fulfill the purpose of your sermon.

Chapter 12

The Preparation to Preach

As the preacher of the day, you will need to have several things in place before you go to the pulpit to deliver your sermon. First, you will need to write the sermon down in full (which the exercises in the past chapters have been gradually helping you develop). This exercise involves writing down everything you plan to say on the pulpit. Writing down your sermon is a safeguard against going off on tangents as you speak. You must make the decision about what you will say long before you preach it. Writing down what you plan to say is a part of that process. Avoid spontaneous, off-the-cuff remarks as much as possible, unless you are absolutely sure those remarks fit well within the process of your sermon. As tempting as those remarks appear to be, they could quite easily take away from your original intention of preaching the counsel of God deposited on your heart during your preparation. I do not, however, assume God cannot speak through spontaneity. I believe he can. But go for spontaneity only when you are sure it is the direction God wants you to take. Just the same, writing down your sermon in full is important. This includes writing down your introduction, the transition into the main points, the explanation of the text of Scripture tied to the main points, the illustration of that point, the application and your conclusion. You will also need to write down your transitions between points, exactly how you plan to execute them.

Once you have written down your sermon, the next process is that of learning it. This second stage may sound awkward. What does learning your sermon really mean if the sermon already came from you, the preacher? It simply means really knowing the sermon in such a way that you will not have to rely on your notes when you go to the pulpit to preach it. In short, memorize your sermon. Preaching your sermon from memory mimics the prophets of the Old Testament as they stood before the people they addressed. Memorizing your sermon gives you enough flexibility to adjust it as necessary from the pulpit. It allows you to know what to say and when to say it. It also allows you to edit the sermon mentally as you proclaim it based on unforeseeable situations in the service, which could range from prior events in the program chopping off some of your preaching time, to specific interruptions during the service such as people walking out or telephones ringing. All these could be distracting to the message. Memorizing your sermon also helps you own the sermon in a way reading it does not.

One Sunday morning, I had written out my sermon in full, but I had not memorized it. I made the mistake of not collating the pages of the sermon. The pages got mixed up in the process, and I forgot to inspect them before going to the pulpit. To my shock and horror, I discovered this problem as I was reading the sermon, with all eyes of the congregation glued to me. I was in trouble because as I read the pages from the pulpit during the preaching, what I said did not make sense at all. I could tell, from the faces of the people in the congregation, that they were as confused as I was, based on what I was saying. It was obvious I had mixed up my points. They were forgiving, though. I paused for a moment and quickly gathered myself together and re-arranged the pages as I spoke spontaneously about what I was saying.

I know of preachers who go around this problem by typing their sermons into a device, such as a tablet or a laptop. This way of preparation certainly helps. However, it comes with its own set of problems. You must make sure your device is fully charged. You must also make sure the device is in a "do not disturb" mode so no one calls or texts you as you speak. Though quite rare, the device could also crash on you or begin an automatic update while you are on the pulpit. Bear in mind what you do is a spiritual battle, and the enemy could capitalize on all these possibilities. To avoid them, do the prior work of memorizing your sermon. It helps boost your confidence on the pulpit. Besides, memorizing the sermon will be possible for you because the ideas are already implanted in you. You will be the human author of the sermon, and you will be thinking through what you plan to say.

Still, if memorizing the sermon word for word sounds difficult to do, then do the next best thing: memorize the ideas in each segment. For example, memorize the big idea in the explanation, memorize the big idea in the illustration, and memorize the big idea in the application. Do this with each point of the sermon. As you transition to the conclusion, memorize the big idea in the conclusion and how you plan to give the final push of that idea. In many cases, this is what I do. But I also memorize the sermon word for word in many more instances. The purpose of all this is simple: not having to rely on your notes. In this way, you will not be crippled on the pulpit should the notes become unavailable for one reason or another.

From committing the sermon to memory or, for that matter, learning it by heart, the third stage is to practice the sermon. This is an absolutely crucial stage of the sermonic process. First, practice the sermon to yourself as if you are preaching the sermon to a live audience. This helps you become well acquainted with the sermon in a way not practicing the sermon does not. Sometimes I do this while sitting by my desk. Other times I do this while standing in my office. I just want to hear how I sound to myself. It also gives me some confidence when I hear, for the first time, how the sermon flows.

Second, practice the sermon in front of a mirror. Observe for yourself how you look like as you preach the sermon. At first this will feel awkward because you will feel as if you are preaching to yourself. But preaching to yourself is exactly what you want to achieve. The sermon ought to make sense to you before you can bring it before your congregation. As you preach to yourself, then, try and determine what you like about your postures, your gestures, your voice inflections and your speaking speed. Take these factors into consideration in your preparation process.

Third and, perhaps most importantly for this stage, practice the sermon in front of a camera and record it in that process. One of my teachers wisely advised me about any art requiring you to be in front of people: "The camera is your best friend and your worst critic." He was right. The camera will not hide from you what you do not like to see. At the same time, however, the camera will help you correct it as you prepare yourself to deliver the sermon. Also, you could quite conceivably bypass the stage of practicing in front of a mirror and go straight to practicing your sermon in front of a video camera. In the past, having a video camera was beyond reach for many people. In this day and age, many people have smart phones with cameras. Recording yourself as you practice is a possibility for many people. If you do have a camera, use it for this very purpose.

As you practice the sermon, be sure to time it. It helps you to know what sorts of adjustments to make as you prepare yourself for the big event. Do not be surprised if, during your first attempt, you happen to go way beyond the time allotted for your preaching. Do not panic when this happens. Simply decide for yourself what you believe is absolutely crucial in the sermon and cannot be left out, and what you think could be deleted. Preachers do this quite often, and doing so should not be a major issue for you. Once you have decided on what will go into the sermon and what will be left out, then practice the edited version and see how it will come out.

Fourth, if you have confidants or friends you can trust, invite one of them, or all of them, to your practice session. Have them listen to the sermon and offer their piece of advice as potential members of your congregation. Since some of them, you hope, could be the recipients of the word of God you will be preaching to them, they will give you the audience's perspective of your sermon. These friends, however, need to be individuals who stay close to the word of God and take their time with the Lord seriously. This requirement is important because they are in tune with God and can listen to the promptings of the Holy Spirit as they make suggestions for your consideration.

Practicing your sermon prepares you for surprises that could arise during the actual preaching event. Those surprises include interruptions from crying children, the program leader cutting some of your preaching time short, your printer failing to print your sermon notes, and your device failing to work as you deliver your sermon from the notes you have printed on that device. These interruptions have happened to many preachers, leaving some at a loss about what to do. One preacher, for example, forgot all his sermon notes at home. He realized this problem minutes before his time to preach had arrived. The remarks he made were quite profound and, sadly, a painful commentary to the preaching event for most preachers. He said, "I regret to announce that I forgot my sermon notes at home. So, today, I will have to rely on the Holy Spirit!"

I would be deeply troubled if the preacher of the day fails to rely on the Holy Spirit, with or without the sermon notes, for it would mean the sermon is more a work of the flesh rather than the result of the Holy Spirit working in the life of the preacher. Preparing the sermon through memorizing or learning the sermon by heart takes the sermon to a unique level.

Also, learning the sermon by heart helps you to earn the confidence of your audience when they finally hear you preach it. They get the impression you know what you are talking about. It gives them the impression you have taken time to prepare for this event. Further, it gives them the impression you have taken them seriously enough to spend time in the presence of the Lord in your preparation, and are now bringing them the final product of your labor in the power of the Holy Spirit. But we are not done with the preparation for delivery yet. More needs to be said.

Exercise

Learn the sermon you have fully written out from the previous exercises by either memorizing it word for word or memorizing the big idea in each segment of the introduction, explanation, illustration and application of the main points as well as the conclusion.

Chapter 13

The Protection of Your Voice

As you practice your sermon in front of a mirror, or in front of a camera, you will need to pay attention to your mode of delivery. It is not enough to have the right words in place, though using the right words is certainly an important aspect of preaching. Additional aspects of the preaching event need to be in place as you preach. Let me mention one of them here, namely, the various ways you will need to use your voice and take care of it. As I describe the use of voice, however, it will not necessarily be in their order of importance. All of them are just as important. Let me begin with the most obvious one, namely, your voice as your primary instrument.

Your voice is your most important preaching instrument. How you use your voice can make or break your preaching. Protecting your voice for the preaching event is important. One of my lay-leaders knows my weakness in this area. Every Sunday, without fail, he hands me a throat lozenge before I preach. It has become his duty to ensure he takes care of my voice before I preach each Sunday. The lozenges certainly help. But over the years I have come to appreciate the importance of taking care of my voice before I speak and even as I speak.

Several aspects of your voice must be taken into consideration. The first entails speaking with authority. Speaking with authority entails speaking with confidence. You are absolutely confident the message you are presenting is biblically-based because the meaning of each point is tied to Scripture. Speaking with authority also entails speaking with conviction. You are absolutely sure what you convey is the word of God because it comes directly from Scripture. The apostle Peter says, those with the gift of speaking must speak as if they are speaking the very words of God (1 Pet 4:10–11). Speaking with authority also entails speaking with some emotion. You cannot worship without involving your emotion. Since speaking is an integral part of worship, your audience must sense the emotion in your speech. But speaking with emotion does not imply getting into emotionalism. Emotionalism involves manipulating the people's feelings sometimes to hysterical levels, none of which are warranted by Scripture. Thus, speaking with authority is not about the loudness or softness of your voice. Rather, it involves self-confidence in your presentation of the ideas you have been working on during your sermon preparation. In speaking with authority, self-confidence enables you to speak intentionally, deliberately, and clearly enunciating your words in ways your audience will understand.

Second, the speaker also needs to speak audibly. In this day and age of technological advancement, churches investing in the use of sound equipment help their pastors convey their messages audibly. However, even with the availability of such technology, some preachers still struggle with projecting their voices. As a speaker, you need to work on the technique of projecting your voice loudly enough to be heard by your audience. Without proper voice projection, the preaching event becomes somewhat of a failure. Projecting your voice in a way that reaches the person at the last pew of the building is the ideal you aim for.

Third, you must control your voice. In other words, you must strike a balance between ensuring everyone hears you and ensuring you do not shout. In other words, you must control your voice. I have learned this fact the hard way. Failure to control my voice has led me to get hoarse. I then lose it in the process of my sermon delivery long before the sermon is over. Avoid shouting in your preaching. Room certainly exists for raising your voice at some points in the sermon for emphasis. But the sermon is not about shouting throughout. It becomes distracting and sometimes offensive to your audience when you shout throughout the sermon.

I sat through a sermon where the preacher of the day was literally screaming at the audience. For him, screaming implied the anointing of the Holy Spirit was on him. The scream was, obviously, not necessary and, certainly, a major obstruction to his communication. It was not clear what he was trying to convey, and no one seemed to know what he was preaching about. By the end of the sermon, everyone seemed thankful it was over.

But I also sat through another sermon where the preacher spoke one sentence very slowly, paused for ten to fourteen seconds before he made his next statement. He did so for forty-five minutes. Sitting through that sermon was painful because his tone of voice was also very low, completely the opposite of the loud and screaming preacher. When this soft-voice speaker was done, everybody in the room gave an audible sigh of relief, specifically because it was a funeral sermon, and the low-voiced sermon simply inflicted more pain on the audience. Obviously, we must strike a balance between these two kinds of extremes.

As you practice your sermon, learn exactly where you want to raise your voice, and where you wish to lower your voice and where you intend to place your voice inflections. Make all of these moves for the purpose of maintaining the attention of your audience throughout the preaching event. Whether you raise your voice or lower it, do so for dramatic effect. Practice both of them over and over until using them becomes second nature. The message gets across more effectively in this way. Your use of your voice is an important part of your preaching calling.

The fourth aspect of your speaking involves maintaining an economy of words. As you speak, be on the lookout for phrase over-use and word over-use. Words such as "You see. . ." or "Amen" or "like" are okay when used minimally. But when we begin to put them in every sentence during the preaching event, they become a distraction. I sat through a sermon where the preacher of the day repeated the same word so many times until I found myself counting the words. I, unintentionally, stopped listening to the sermon. From the time I counted how many times that word was used to the time the sermon was over, it had been used over one-hundred times. The speaker kept using the word "like" in just about every sentence of the sermon. It became quite a distraction.

Many preachers over-use the word "Amen." Others put it in the wrong place. Whereas in many cases the preacher uses the word to get some kind of affirmation from the audience or to get the audience to stay with him, it can be overused and, sometimes, misused. For example, I heard one preacher say something like this: "Many people are going to hell. . . amen?" I think he meant to say, "Many people are going to hell, isn't that correct?" But "amen?" and "isn't that correct?" have different meanings. Amen means "it is as good as done," and that is why we say "amen" at the end of every prayer. Using "amen" in the way that preacher used it suggests a misunderstanding of its meaning.

As you preach, then, watch your words, watch the volume of your voice and speak with authority. Your voice is your most important preaching instrument. Taking care of it is important. Protecting it from overuse is just as important. Overuse of your voice can sometimes degenerate into a sore throat. As I concluded an intensive class at Asbury Theological Seminary where I teach, I lost my voice. I had been speaking continuously as I lectured my students for three and a half days non-stop from 8 am to 5 pm. By the end of the lecture, I had lost my voice. The following day I had a preaching event. My voice was hoarse, and my throat was sore. I still went onto the pulpit and delivered the word of God, which I believed God had placed in my heart. It was quite a painful experience. Clearly, I had not taken care of my voice. I was exhausted by the end of the day, and my voice needed a rest. I had not taken care of my voice that week. Regaining the full use of my voice took about three days.

As a preacher, once your voice is gone, your preaching ministry is over. That is why you must take care of it every day of your life. If someone invites you, for example, to preach in a convention each day for five days, then you know you have a massive task ahead of you. Taking care of your voice at that time becomes your top priority. Preaching can be very strenuous to your voice. It taxes your voice quite considerably. But if you take care of your voice, you will serve the Lord well with this blessed instrument.

Chapter 14

The Problem of Distractions

As YOU PREACH, SEVERAL aspects of your presentation, besides the sermon delivery, need to be taken into consideration: hand gestures, body posture, pacing on the pulpit, facial expressions and your outfit. Let's begin with the first one, namely, gestures. The use of gestures is an integral part of preaching. Gestures facilitate the communication of the message of the gospel by helping to emphasize certain points you, as the preacher, want to put across. No specific rules exist for the use of gestures. They simply result from the preacher's personality and from how the preacher has used them over the years. Culturally speaking, however, certain gestures communicate specific messages depending on how one was raised.

A thumbs-up sign, for example, may convey a certain message in one culture and a completely different message in another culture. In Bangladesh, the use of the thumbs-up gesture is considered an insult. In most Western countries, the use of it is a sign of approval. In the Philippines, the "come here" gesture with your index finger repeatedly as a way of bidding someone to step forward toward you is not a welcome sign. The sign is used to beckon dogs, and not human beings. In the Western countries, it seems acceptable, though some still find it rude. Therefore, you need to be culturally sensitive and aware of your context before you use certain gestures on the pulpit. In the West, joining the tip of your index finger with the tip of your thumb in the same hand conveys the idea everything is okay. In Brazil, doing so is rude. President Richard Nixon learned this truth the hard way in the 1950s when he went to Brazil.

The point I make is simple. Be aware of the meaning of certain gestures as you preach your sermon. Be sure the gestures you use convey your intended meaning, and be sure to use gestures your audience accepts. Some congregations find the gesture of index-finger pointing directly toward them deeply insulting. This fact seems to escape the notice of many preachers as they use their fingers to emphasize certain points during the course of their sermon. If you must point, open your hand, keep your palms facing down and use all your fingers pointing in one direction as you draw attention to what you wish your audience to see.

Also, gesture overuse interferes with the delivery of the sermon. Repeated finger pointing throughout the sermonic process will certainly affect the attention of your audience. One of my former professors had this habit whenever he preached. He always stuck to his handwritten sermon notes, and wagged his index finger upward toward the roof to press his point. He seemed to do that at every sentence. I got so amused by this gesture every time I saw him preach. Much later in my studies, he alternated that gesture with a karate chop on the podium. Again, he did it quite repeatedly. If he was not karate-chopping the podium, he was merely karate-chopping the air. I had no problem watching him do this once or twice, or even four times during his sermon delivery. But when he did it repeatedly, I began to notice of it.

When you record yourself practicing your sermon, be on the lookout, therefore, for gesture overuse. Doing so requires you to watch your recorded sermon in its entirety. Merely watching the first few minutes of your sermon delivery is not sufficient to reveal any overuse of your gestures. It requires you to watch yourself from the beginning of the sermon until the end of the recording. The more you guard against this habit, the more you eliminate at least one factor that could interfere with your sermon delivery.

Closely related to gesture overuse is the aspect of your posture. The preacher's posture is an important part of the delivery process as the verbal presentation of the sermon. Watch your posture. Your posture on the pulpit needs to be consistent with the preaching event itself. When you keep your head in a drooping position, you will be conveying a negative message to your audience—a message implying a lack of confidence on your part. What professors of preaching recommend in this instance is a posture conveying a sense of confidence and authority—and it should! You have taken the time to pray and prepare for the message. You have taken the time to write the message out in full. You have memorized the message or learned chunks of it by heart. It has now become a part of you. You own the message. It is time now to convey it to your audience. Do so with authority and conviction. Maintain eye contact with your audience, and proclaim that message the Lord has given you. With your feet firmly planted on the floor and your hands ready to help you in the preaching event, let the message ring out from you and proclaim it with authority.

Some preachers like to pace from one side of the pulpit to the other. I cautiously recommend this. When you move from one side of the pulpit to another, it helps you, as the preacher, to be relaxed and overcome the tension preachers sometimes face. It also does the same for the audience. It helps them to see you are not overly tied to your sermon notes, and that you are, in fact, preaching from the very core of your being. However, this can also be a distraction if overused. I have seen it getting overused. At a revival service I was a part of while pastoring a church in Lexington, Kentucky, the preacher of the day went back and forth on the pulpit. But that was not enough for him. He climbed onto one of the chairs in the sanctuary, jumped down and sat on it, and began riding it like a horse! What he was trying to demonstrate or illustrate was not clear. Just the same, I could not believe my eyes as the preaching event unfolded. The congregation was quite amused about this. It seemed he was trying to manipulate a revival into being or something to that effect.

One other aspect the preachers must be cautious about is their facial expression. Facial expressions are windows into your emotions. You must give your audience an expression they believe invites them into the preaching event. Facial expressions must be consistent with the mood and the tone of the sermon. But just as important, a scowl is not quite an inviting expression for a preacher to have, unless the preacher is dealing with a very serious matter requiring righteous anger, of the sort that prompted Jesus to cleanse the temple or of the kind that prompted the apostle Paul to command his readers to expel the immoral brother. Generally speaking, however, the preacher ought to invite members of his audience into the preaching event using a facial expression consistent with the mood of the sermon.

Obviously, preachers must learn to control their movements on the pulpit. If you are a preacher, and you have substance in your sermon, the audience will know it. You do not have to manipulate your audience in your attempt to attain certain ends possibly unwarranted by the text under consideration. The attempt to get dramatic must be done with caution to avoid taking away from the message you bring from hours of preparation. Practicing your sermon goes a long way in helping you guard against these pitfalls.

A final area that could be a distraction for the preacher is the preacher's outfit. I was trained in a conservative school that always required the preacher to wear a coat and tie or a suit and tie. I have stuck to that tradition throughout my preaching career. I do so out of respect for the preaching event, for God's people and, of course, for God himself. However, commitment to this practice is not to say preachers dressed casually on the pulpit are sinning against God. Some contexts feel a sense of connection with casually dressed preachers than with smartly dressed ones. What the preacher must bear in mind is to avoid outfits that become a distraction to the proclaimed message.

I attended a conference where the preacher of the day was overly dressed for the service. He wore a bright red suit, a bright red shirt, a bright red tie, and bright red shoes. Whatever he wore took away from the sermonette he gave. Everything was shining. All I could remember was the redness of the preacher. I could not remember his sermon. It was quite a sight to see. The rule of thumb is simple: what you wear must be completely free of distraction so that the message God has given you can be conveyed without hindrance.

Preaching, therefore, takes more than mere verbal proclamation. It takes more than the delivery of a sermon or the conveying of an idea from the pulpit. The preacher must look into the additional aspects mentioned here. Ironically, without the sermon, there will be no preaching. But even with the preaching event in place, failure to take these other aspects into consideration undercuts the sermon delivery process, which, in turn undercuts the full purpose of the gospel message. You, the preacher, must take all these aspects into consideration as you prepare for the preaching event. One more aspect, which cannot be overlooked, is the aspect of prayer. It is the final item in the preparation process. To this we now turn.

Chapter 15

The Praying Part

ALLOW ME TO SHARE with you my personal experiences in praying for my Sunday sermon preparation process. Because I am quite aware of the spiritual warfare involved in the process of sermon preparation, I do my best to ensure I remain in the right spiritual wavelength for the preaching ministry God has placed in my hand. The way I do this is by fasting and prayer. I do a dry fast every Friday of the month to keep me focused on what is coming on any given Sunday. Fasting does me a lot of spiritual good. One of the things it does for me is sensitizing my awareness of the presence of God in my life. The more I fast, the more I am reminded of what lies ahead of me. The more I feel hungry during the day, the more I remember I am setting myself aside for a spiritual purpose, namely, the purpose of delivering God's word on a given Sunday.

I note, though, that on some occasions I fall into the temptation of losing the point of what I am trying to do, even when I am fasting. One does not merely fast for the sake of fasting. One fasts in order to pray in a more focused way. The day I fail to pray during my fasting period is the day I actually lose focus of the spiritual goals I believe God is calling me to achieve. As a minister and a seminary professor, my life gets quite busy. I find myself having to answer calls, having to grade papers, having to post assignments for my students, and having to do everything that needs to be done, and forgetting the important discipline of prayer.

One could, quite conceivably, construe what I have just described here as the enemy's attempt to draw me away from the discipline of praying for the Sunday sermon. Whereas I do not want to be involved in what C. S. Lewis called an unhealthy interest in seeing demons behind every bush, I still note that this kind of forgetfulness, forgetfulness to bathe the sermon in prayer during the fasting period, remains at the heart of spiritual warfare, with the enemy winning if we remain prayerless, and with us winning if we maintain our prayer vigil. The believer is always at war with the enemy, ranging from temptations to be prayerless to temptations to violate God's commands willingly and rebelliously. For this reason, you and I need to maintain our prayer vigil against these forces of evil.

Here, then, is how I overcome this. The moment I begin to feel hungry, I take that as God's call to prayer. When I feel hungry during my fasting period, I walk into my prayer closet and, calling it my spiritual lunch or spiritual dinner, I surrender the day to the Lord and lift up the purpose of my fast before the Lord. I ask God specifically to give me his word for his people for the coming Sunday. I seek his guidance and direction in my process of preparation to deliver his word. But I also confess all known and unknown sins in my life before the Lord. I ask him to fill me afresh with his Spirit and empower me to pray throughout the day as I wait on him to deliver his word into my heart. Each time God has come through for me without fail, provided I take the time to fast in this way. Each time God has given me a word, including a word I initially thought was innocuous and powerless. By the time I am done preaching, God's word finally connects with the audience in ways beyond my imagination.

Fasting is something the preacher should do regularly, that is, if you are capable of doing it. On several occasions I have fasted for longer periods of time, seeking God's guidance and direct intervention in pressing matters near and dear to my heart. During those extended periods of fasting, I literally felt the presence of the

Lord. I have no biblical reference to describe this experience, but I did feel as if I was immersed in the sea of divine presence. That description is the best I could ever give. By the time the fasting is over, a sense of righteous grief overwhelms me because I realize I would not be sensing that presence until I go back into that extended period of fasting. Fasting does, indeed, prepare the heart of the preacher in powerful ways for the preaching and proclamation of the word of God. I also need to mention that God did show up in remarkable ways during and after that fasting period.

Having pointed this out, I quickly note that fasting is not for everyone. Individuals with serious medical conditions should not attempt to fast unless cleared by their doctor. If you are such an individual, seek medical advice first, before embarking on the exercise of fasting. Failure to do so could result in serious health consequences. Strangely, some individuals I knew had medical conditions chose to fast on one occasion in the past, and trusted God to lead them through the process without seeking medical advice. God was merciful to them. They did not experience any serious or significant health repercussions. Seemingly, God stood by them and helped them finish the fasting period without incident. Whereas this is commendable, Scripture also warns us against putting the Lord to the test. Unless you are absolutely sure God wants you to go that direction, avoid having a fast that fails to seek medical advice from your physician.

I also mention how, at the beginning of each year, my wife and I and, sometimes, our son (when he wants to), go into a fast of some kind for the purpose of starting the year on the right spiritual foot. We decide whether the fast will be a vegetable only fast, or whether it will be a squeezed juice only fast. Each experience is unique in its own way. Our goal, during such fasts, is to be in the right spiritual wavelength for the rest of the year as we tackle some of the things the year will bring our way. Fasting is very much a part of my life as a preacher.

A prepared sermon is great. A prepared heart with a prepared sermon is a potent weapon against the kingdom of the enemy. Prayer is your best preparation for the preaching event. Without prayer, a sermon turns into a theological lecture. Of course, I find nothing wrong with giving theological lectures if offered in a forum set aside for lectures. But when a sermon becomes a dry lecture, it lacks power. Prayer gives the sermon the power it is supposed to have. As one who has preached numerous sermons over the years, I can tell when the sermon is dry, bereft of the Spirit's power. You, the preacher, must not overlook this important piece of the preaching puzzle—praying throughout the process of preparation.

First, assuming your minister has not given you a topic to speak about or a text to speak about, ask God to lead you to the right topic and to the right text. Be open to God's guidance and direction in this area. Quite possibly, you might have a burden in your heart about a topic you feel needs to be addressed. That's a very good indication God has put the burden in you. It is a very good indication the Holy Spirit wants you to address that topic. Begin seeking God's guidance on what text of Scripture best addresses that topic, and how you would go about outlining it.

Alternatively, your minister could give you a topic to speak about, and possibly even the text itself. In such situations, be open to the very likely possibility that God gave your minister that topic, and the minister likely believes in your ability to address it. Receive it with humility and begin praying for guidance and direction on how to handle the text or the topic. As you pray, always be specific, asking God to give you a word for his people. I have done this many times in the past, and God has always come through. He has never let me down.

Once you have settled on a text, ask God to guide you through the process of deciding on the theme of the text. The theme is always based on what you derive from the text. Remember, the theme is a full sentence expressing a biblical truth. The truth may be a description of a state of affairs such as the following: Jesus wants to meet our needs; or God loves you; or prayer works. The truth may also be a call to a certain kind of action—obedience, evangelism, prayer, discipleship, worship, and so on. Examples include calls of the following sorts: bring your burdens to Jesus, or be a disciple of Jesus, or walk away from sinful desires, and so on. Be sure your theme comes directly from the text in a way that summarizes the entire passage of the text in one interpretive statement. As you study the text, ask God to guide you in determining the theme of the text.

If, however, you have wrestled with a specific burden in your heart, and you already have a text you have selected to address that burden, then go for that text. As already noted, God, quite likely, put that burden in your heart. I have experienced these kinds of situations numerous times in my ministry. The burden, for example, came during my quiet time with the Lord, and as I read his word, he gave me a theme and main points from a given text. Both the theme and the main points flowed quite naturally from the text, eventually leading me to a specific word for a specific group of people needing to hear that word at precisely that time.

During your time of prayer, ask yourself what your general purpose will be and what your specific purpose will look like. The burden in your heart will go a long way in helping you to determine the nature of that purpose. God, quite likely, wants to do something special through you among your target audience, and the burden he has placed in your heart will help you decide what purpose you intend to achieve through that preaching event.

Pray, also, through the process of deciding what the main point is, or what the main points are. Having only one point from the text is absolutely possible. Also, having more than four or five points is quite possible. On one occasion, I preached a seven-point sermon, which was quite demanding. This demand came from the fact that I had to squeeze seven points within a span of thirty minutes, forcing me to give each segment of the sermon, from the introduction to the conclusion, an average of three minutes each. I was exhausted by the time I was done preaching on that day.

I have also been in situations where I looked at the text but was unable to determine what the main point was. On one such occasion (and there have been many), I stared at the text and it seemed to stare back at me. At that point, I realized I had not surrendered the text to the Lord for guidance and direction. After quickly confessing my sin of not lifting that need to the Lord, I asked for guidance and direction on how I would go about deriving the outline from the text. Very quickly, God made the outline clear to me.

At other times, even after praying for guidance and direction about outlining the text, I could not get any sense of direction. On one such occasion, it took me a whole week to come up with the outline. What I realized was going on, though, was the fact that God just wanted me to remain in his presence as I took in every word of that text and learned it by heart. When I sensed that this was the direction the Lord was taking me, I was more at ease with the process, and I was able to receive an outline from God by reading the text.

Bear in mind that praying for the outline comes as you study the text using the resources available to you—commentaries, study Bibles, concordances and your personal reflection on what the text is about. Ask the Lord to illuminate your mind as you read through those resources to get the intended meaning of each text. A sermon text bathed in prayer in this way will not fail to connect with the audience as they listen to the presentation God has given you. The more you spend time in prayer over your sermon preparation, the more powerful God's visit upon his people will be.

Once your outline is in place, ask for God's guidance as you put your introduction together. Ask him to help you position the introduction in a way that gets the attention of your audience. What words will you use and how will you go about getting the attention of God's people during this process? That question should be at the forefront in your prayers. How should you create a need among the people, giving them every reason to listen to the message God has given you? Again, that question should be at the forefront in your prayers. The point is this: pray through the sermon writing process.

As you populate your first point with the relevant explanation, ask God to give you the necessary explanatory power to make the text come alive. Once again, what you have gathered from the commentaries, from the study Bibles, from the concordances, and from the word studies, should come in handy. But just as important as the facts you have gathered from your study are, how you explain what you have gathered will matter to your listeners. Be clear in telling your audience what that text means. You will need to ask God's guidance for such clarity. He will surely give you the relevant explanatory words.

As you get to the illustration stage, your sermon will take a different turn. It will be the creative turn of your work. Here is where your personality as a preacher gets factored into the sermon. God has already factored you into this process. But you will still need to seek his help at this stage. You will need to ask him to give you an illustration that does not overshadow the text, but helps to enhance its meaning. You will need to ask him to give you an illustration that does not under-explain the text either. Whatever illustrations you use, ask God to help you ensure they make the intended meaning of the text clearer. Once you have written out your illustrations, you are ready for the next stage.

The application stage is a crucial part of the sermonic process. This stage helps to answer the "So what?" question of your entire sermon. It is where you issue the call to action. It is where you challenge your audience to make the necessary changes. It is where you issue the call to repentance if your message is salvific. Absolutely essential is the prayer you lift to God for the right words to use during this stage. Ask for his help in this process and write the words that come to mind, being sure that what you are writing is exactly in the neighborhood of what God wants you to say on the pulpit. The more you spend time in prayer during the writing stage, the more he will honor his word to come to you and empower you with his living word. Once you have written down the explanation, illustration and application for every point, you will be transitioning to the conclusion.

As with the application, the conclusion helps you create the final push for the purpose of your message. It is where you offer the summary of your main points. In many cases, it is the climax of what your sermon is all about. Pray through the process of writing the conclusion. Do you sense God leading you to make an altar call? Ask God for guidance and direction on that. I do not always

sense God leading me to make an altar call when I preach. Sometimes, during my preaching, I get the impression he wants me to
make an altar call and give his people an opportunity to respond.
On other occasions, after giving my sermons a second look, I end
up believing I do not need to make an altar call, and then, as I
deliver the sermon, I get a very strong impression to make the altar
call, and I go ahead and do it, as if there was a change of mind on
my part.

Once you have prayed through the writing process, you need
to pray during the learning process. Ask him to help you remember everything you have written down, whether you choose to remember it word for word, or you choose to remember it in terms
of the big ideas in each segment of your sermon. Once you believe
you have learned the sermon by heart, you are ready to practice
it, either in front of a mirror or before your phone's video camera.
As with the memorizing part, and before you begin practicing the
sermon, ask God for his strength to help you practice it well, and
pray just as you would normally pray before you begin preaching
the sermon in a real-life situation. Upon completing your practice,
determine for yourself whether you are happy with how the sermon has turned out. If you are happy with it, be thankful to God
for leading you through every stage of your sermon preparation. If
you are not happy with it, figure out what your areas of improve-
ment are, and how you need to correct them.

Also, if you choose to have your confidants listen to the presentation you have prepared, seek their pieces of advice. Be sure
these confidants are people you can trust, people who can give you
constructive criticism, and not people who will pull you away from
saying what you believe the Lord has placed in your heart. However, if they give you good biblical reasons to adjust your message
in one way rather than in the way you intended to present it, then
you have good reasons to listen to them. As you pray during this
process, include them in your prayers.

On the day of your preaching event, gather your close confidants together and have them surround you with prayers shortly
before the service. Some churches normally gather before service

to pray for the worship event. If this kind of set-up is available in your preaching venue, take advantage of it. The worship service itself, however, normally presents unforeseeable challenges for the preacher. Your well-wishers in the service will try to get your attention, and that intention could take your focus off your sermon, if you are not well-prepared. Their presence there should also be an encouragement to you because they have come to support you in your attempt to fulfill God's calling for you in your life at that time. Acknowledge their presence with a friendly wave or a nod and then take your seat.

When your sermon time comes, be sure to lift the sermon to the Lord in prayer before the congregation and ask him to speak to everyone present in the congregation. You need not have an extended prayer during this time because you have been praying over the sermon for the past couple of days. Once you complete your prayer, the time for delivering God's word to his people has come. Speak with authority. Speak with conviction. Speak with confidence. Upon the completion of your sermon, be sure to thank God for having walked you through the sermonic process from beginning to end. Also, at the end of that very day, take the time to thank God for using you throughout the sermon.

Chapter 16

The Bird's Eye-View

HERE IS A SUMMARY of what I have presented from the very first page. The purpose of this chapter is to put together, in a bird's eye-view, the principles hitherto articulated. I believe when you grasp this summary, it will place the principles of this method at your fingertips. Of course, one will have to read the whole book to understand the summary I present here. But once you understand the summary so presented, you will not need to re-read the whole book. I make this claim because you will have grasped the principles not merely by reading them, but also by putting them into practice. Assuming you have been consistent with your prayer life and have done your devotions faithfully, the question to ask is: in a nutshell, what is the starting point?

Identify the Text

Your first order of sermonic business is to identify the text you will use for your sermon. Without a text, you really have no sermon, since every preaching of the word must be based on the text of Scripture. In your early stages of preaching, using a text with three to six verses will be helpful. You will not feel too overwhelmed by having to do a lot of explanation in your explanation stage. However, if you believe you can handle more than six verses, go for it. A six-verse text is sufficient for the method of expository preaching I present here. You could also use multiple texts for your points, giving each point a separate text of Scripture, linking them together because they address the same idea. For an illustration of this possibility, see sermon sample number three published in Chapter 19 of this book.

Identify the Title

Once you have identified the text, your next task would be to identify the title of your sermon from the text. The title could be a one-word title, such as: trust, faith, grace, salvation, hope, patience, kindness, goodness, love, faithfulness, gentleness, joy, or peace. The title could also be a multiple-word title such as: self-control, loving God, faithful giving, brotherly love, Christian discipleship, saving grace, or the resurrection of Jesus. The text, though, should help determine your sermon title. Be sure the title is clear in your mind. If it is not clear in your mind, it will not be clear in the mind of your audience. Thus, have a clearly worded title for your sermon.

State Your Purpose

Stating your purpose from the beginning is an important and crucial stage in the process of your sermon preparation. The purpose of your sermon gives you the reason why you believe anyone should listen to what you have to share with your audience. Be sure to state for yourself what the general purpose is. Will it be to inform, to challenge, or to encourage? Once you have done so, you will then be more specific about your particular purpose. The particular purpose is more pointed, and custom made for the specific audience you will be addressing. In your specification of the particular purpose, it will become clearer once your theme and main points have been developed. The general purpose, however, should remain firmly in place. Bear in mind that the theme and main points are an extension of your particular purpose.

Formulate Your Theme

The theme of your sermon is a full sentence expressing a theological truth or a full sentence challenging the audience to action of some kind based on the Bible. The action could be a challenge to obey a specific command articulated in Scripture, or to refrain from a particular sin, or to live their lives in a certain way. The theological truth could be something such as: the Christian life is a challenge; God loves you; Jesus is our Savior; and so on. What you must remember about the theme is that an ideal theme should not be longer than seven words. The purpose of keeping it this short is to help your audience remember it. If the theme is too long, members of your audience will have a hard time trying to recollect what it was. Keep your theme as short as possible. Also, bear in mind that the theme summarizes your sermon text in seven words or less. The theme, therefore, is an interpretive statement of your sermon text. It must come from the Bible.

Develop the Main Points

Develop the main points of your sermon by looking at what the text says. As you develop those points, link them with the text. Your text might just have one point, or it might be a multiple point text. As you develop your points, keep an eye on how you will explain it. Develop each point and state each point in a simple but memorize-able way. Be sure your point is not too long. When the point is too long, you will have a hard time remembering it, and your audience will also struggle to recall it. Once your main points are fully developed, return to your purpose statement and write it out in full including in it your theme and main points.

Compose Your Introduction

Your introduction is the entry point of your sermon. A good introduction gets the attention of your audience. The attention span of your audience could be rather short if you do not introduce your sermon creatively. One way to do this is to begin with an interesting story, or with a catchy phrase or a punchline, or a profound remark made by some famous person. A good introduction creates a need. It creates a need by drawing the attention of the audience to a specific area of concern, or a specific topic of interest, or something most members of the audience are dealing with in their lives, for which they seek a solution. Your introduction will create an anticipation in the lives of the audience for a possible solution or guidance and direction on how they can handle the issue in question. A good introduction gives the audience the general direction of the sermon, and how you plan to proceed in the preaching event. It makes the audience know that the sermon has a sense of direction, thereby enabling them to want to walk with you through your sermonic process. Fourth, a good introduction transitions smoothly into the main points or, stated differently, into the main sermon body.

Explain Your Points

After introducing your sermon, your task is to explain the text. As already noted, here is where your research through the commentaries, study Bibles, word studies and concordances come in handy. You will be tying together everything you have garnered from studying the text and putting it into one cohesive whole for each point. If you have the ability to look at the text in the original languages, this will be an added advantage. But be careful not to say the Greek words or the Hebrew words from the pulpit. It puts you seriously at risk of losing your audience. It interferes with the train of thought of your audience. Besides, very few of your members, if any, will remember the Greek or Hebrew words you will use on the pulpit. Be simple in your explanation without compromising the contents of the text.

Illustrate The Text

From explaining the text under the first point, illustrate the text under the first point. Your illustration could come from specific true-to-life stories, or from illustration books, or from newspaper clippings, or from published stories or even from your published stories. Your illustrations could include skits and drama using members of your audience for the cast. Of course, the assumption is you have prepared well in advance for this event long before you use it on the pulpit. Your illustration could also include a piece of music, which you can play if you are a gifted musician, or you could ask your church musician to play it, or you could have your sound technician play it through the church's sound system. The purpose of your illustration is to enhance the meaning of the text. Be careful, therefore, that your illustration does not overshadow the text, or under-explain it either. It should be in the neighborhood of making the text clearer to the audience.

Apply The Text

Once you have explained and illustrated the text under the first, second or third point (depending on the number of points your sermon has), you need to apply the text. Here is where you ask the question, "How does it work?" Specifically, "How does it work for me?" Here is where the purpose of your sermon begins to get fulfilled. At this stage, you issue the call to action that will get the members of your audience to begin to act in a transformational way. At this point, you are making a pitch for change, or issuing a call for salvation, or encouraging a move toward repentance, or offering comfort to the bereaved—all of these based on the text of Scripture.

Conclude Your Sermon

Once you have explained, illustrated and applied every point of your sermon, you will transition to the conclusion. The conclusion summarizes the main points of the sermon. Your conclusion, also, makes the final and more intentional call to action. It is where you issue the challenge to your audience to make the move they need to make in order to be where God wants them to be. At this stage, the altar call is issued if you feel God is leading you in that direction. Once you have completed these two duties in the altar call, you will end the sermon in a word of prayer.

In a nutshell, then, the pages of this chapter give you a summary of what this entire book is all about. Once you get familiar with these ingredients, and learn how to use them, designing a sermon based on this style of preaching should come easily. Moreover, you will be on your way to preaching engaging sermons that will connect with your audience all the time. In the next chapters, you will have sample sermons that will, hopefully, illustrate the process I have been describing throughout this book, with the exception of including the outline page for formatting purposes, and of using letters for my points rather than Roman numerals. I simply begin with the introduction of the sermon and proceed to the conclusion. As you read the sermons, and hopefully develop your own, I sincerely and honestly pray you will become a seasoned preacher in the coming days, even if you have never been to seminary.

Chapter 17

Sample Sermon One
Introduction (Hebrews 11:1, 2)

SOMEONE ONCE SAID, "ALL you've got is not faith until faith is all you've got!" I have to confess this statement got my attention. How much faith do you need to have in order to sense God's divine presence, or God's divine power, or God's divine provision in your life? When do you know you have enough faith in your life? And what do we mean when we say we have faith in God? Faith, in the Bible, really means "taking God at his word."

The line I quoted at the very beginning of my remarks tells you how faith is absolutely crucial for living the Christian life. The topic of faith in the Bible is quite intriguing, if you ask me. It is intriguing in the sense that in many instances in the Bible, God or, for that matter, Jesus, would not make a desired move unless those for whom the move was made were absolutely confident about God's ability to make that move.

For example, in Matt 9:27 and 28, two blind men cried out to Jesus for mercy saying, "Son of David, have mercy on us!" Before Jesus could heal them, he asked, "Do you believe I can do this?" And they answered, "Yes, Lord." He then touches their eyes, and with these remarkable words he says, "According to your faith, be it done unto you."

Prior to that story, a sick woman touches the hem of Jesus' garment quite secretly, until Jesus turns around and asks, "Who touched me?" The woman, realizing she could not go unnoticed, identifies herself and begins to tell the story of how she was healed. Jesus then says, "Take heart, Daughter! Your faith has healed you!"

On another occasion, Jesus tells his disciples that if they had faith as small as a mustard seed, they could tell a mountain to be cast into the sea and it would be done unto them. These examples, plus numerous other examples in Scripture, tell us that faith is absolutely crucial to seeing God working in your life.

Faith is when you take God at his word. Faith is when you trust God to do what he says he will do. Faith is when you believe that God will in fact do what he has promised to do. One major reason God chooses not to work in our midst is when we doubt him. When we doubt him, we make him out to be a liar. His word says, without faith it is impossible to please God.

But the Bible expects us to have faith in God. This is because faith is our source of divine confidence. Faith is our source of divine conviction. Faith is our source of divine commendation.

Faith is Our Source of Divine Confidence (1a)

Faith is our source of divine confidence. The Bible says, in Hebrews 11:1: "Faith is being sure of what we hope for." In other words, taking God at his word is being confident that what we hope for will come to pass. Trusting the promises of God is anticipating those promises will be fulfilled. Believing the word of God means you have unwavering confidence his word will come true in your life.

I wonder if you've heard about the story of a prayer meeting that was called somewhere in a midwestern town of the United States. It was a prayer meeting called for by an interdenominational gathering specifically because they had experienced months of blistering heat and drought, and the farmers there needed divine intervention. They needed to pray for rain. Everyone who came to the prayer meeting, came wearing sun-glasses. This little girl, however, walked into the prayer meeting with her umbrella ready.

If we are going to pray for rain, she thought, I'd better prepare for it with my umbrella.

Brothers and sisters, the church of Jesus Christ is suffering from epistemic anemia. It is a lack of knowledge and trust that God will do whatever he has promised. It is a lack of confidence that God can do today the very things he did two thousand years ago through his Son Jesus Christ and through his disciples. A severe drought exists of God doing his work in our midst. No wonder the world thinks what Christians believe is all a fairy tale. We need to regain that divine confidence in God. I know of no other way except to trust God wholeheartedly that he will do what he promises and he stands behind his word to fulfill it. Faith is our source of divine confidence.

Faith is Our Source of Divine Conviction (1b)

Faith is our source, not only of divine confidence, but also of our divine conviction. The Bible says "Faith is being sure of what we hope for and certain of what we do not see." In other words, faith implies a conviction of a certain truth even if it is not immediately evident to our senses. The original text there gives you the impression that you are convicted of the truth of what you do not see, not merely with your eyes, but what you do not perceive immediately with your senses. In other words, even if you have not seen it, even if you have not sensed it, even if you have not touched it, you are confident that the thing in question is true, it is real, it is authentic specifically because God said it.

Let me disabuse you of what faith is not. Faith is not believing something you know is not true. Faith does not imply believing a lie. Faith implies believing the truth of God even if the truth is not immediately accessible to your eyes.

Michael Green describes a situation that took place near the end of the Second World War. Members of the Allied forces were often found searching farms and houses for snipers. One abandoned house had been reduced to rubble. The house had a basement and the searchers found their way into that basement. On a crumbling wall, a victim of the Holocaust had drawn the Star of David, possibly using a hard sharp object like a stone or a piece of metal. Beneath it, the victim wrote, "I believe in the sun, even when it does not shine. I believe in love, even when it is not shown. I believe in God, even when He does not speak."

What I think the victim really meant here was, "I believe in the existence of the sun even when I do not see it shine. I believe in the existence of love even when it has not been shown to me. I believe in God even when he seems to be silent."

Brothers and sisters, that is what faith is all about. Many times, God appears to be silent, in which case we need to walk away from all the noise around us and listen to his voice. Many times, God seems to be hiding. In that case, we need to walk away from all distractions and sense his presence in that little prayer closet. Many times, God's word seems to be failing. But we need to be patient enough to wait on him and see him move. The more we spend time with God, the more we will see his hand where no one else can see it; the more you will hear his voice where no one else can hear it; the more we will feel his presence when no one else can feel it. Faith is our source of divine conviction.

Faith is Our Source of Divine Commendation (2)

Faith is our source, not only of divine confidence or divine conviction. Faith is also our source of of divine commendation. The Bible says in 11:2, "This is what the ancients were commended for." In other words, "Having faith is what the apostles were commended for." Having faith is what the Old Testament saints were commended for. Having this conviction, and having this confidence is what the saints of God were commended for in days gone by. They took God at his word, and they were commended for it. They believed God would do what he promised to do, and they were commended for it. They were praised for it.

I am sure you know that faith is central to all of life. Someone noted how we exercise faith in just about every arena of our lives. For example, you go to a doctor whose name you cannot pronounce and whose degrees and credentials you have never verified. He writes for you a prescription whose contents you cannot read. You take it to a pharmacist you have never met before. The pharmacist then gives you a chemical compound you do not understand. Then you go home and take the pill according to the instructions on the bottle. Green says you do all these in trusting and sincere faith.

Suppose you were skeptical and went back to the doctor and said, "I could not pronounce your name, I have not verified your degrees, I could not understand the prescription, I met the pharmacist for the first time who gave me a chemical I did not know—for that reason, I could not think of putting that pill in my mouth." That is not commendable at all.

But here is a God you know, whose name is "I AM," whose credentials cannot be rivaled, whose prescriptions are easy to understand, who takes you to the Great Physician Jesus Christ, who heals you with a simple touch or a simple word. Surely that counts for something! The ancients were commended for their faith because they followed these guidelines, and thousands upon thousands were saved, the sick were healed, the demons were cast out and the dead were raised. If you want divine commendation from God, maintain your trust in him. If you want approval from God, maintain your faith in him. If you want God to affirm you, take God at his word because faith is a source of divine commendation.

Conclusion

We need some of that today. I dare say, we need all of that today. The starting point is a daily intimate walk with the Lord that builds your faith, not merely going through the motions, but really having a conversation with God where you read his word and hear his voice through the reading of his word. The starting point is praying daily as the apostles did, or praying three times a day as Daniel did, or spending hours communicating with God in your prayer closet as Jesus did. That will build your faith. It will be the faith of the apostles. It will be the faith of the martyrs. It will be the faith of the mustard seed. It will be a messianic faith. It will be a miracle-working faith. It will be the faith that God honors. Faith is our source of divine confidence, of divine conviction and of divine commendation.

Chapter 18

Sample Sermon Two
Introduction (2 Peter 1:1, 2)

A DIFFERENCE EXISTS BETWEEN knowing God and knowing about God. Many people know about God. But not many know God. Knowing about someone is one thing. But knowing someone is another thing altogether. Most of us know about the governor of this state. But fewer of us really know the governor. Most of us know about the president of this country. But fewer of us really know the president. Most of us know about God. But fewer of us really know God.

So, what is the difference between knowing someone and knowing about someone? When you know about someone, that knowledge is factual. But when you know someone, the knowledge is deeper than factual knowledge. It is experiential knowledge. It means you know the person, and the person knows you. It means you know what that person likes and what the person does not like.

For example, the level of knowledge you have for the governor of this state is very different from the level of knowledge you have of your spouse or your brother or your parent. You know members of your family very well. But even if you know your governor, you do not know him quite that well specifically because he likely does not know you. So when you say you know *about* someone, it is quite different than when you say you *actually* know someone.

What about your knowledge of God? No doubt God knows you very, very well. But how well do you know your God? How deep is the level of your knowledge of God? Do you know him enough to say you know anything about God? Do you know him enough to say you have a strong relationship with him? Do you know him as well as you know your spouse? Do you know him as well as you know your siblings? Do you know him as well as you know your children?

When you attain that level of knowledge about God, you begin to have major spiritual convictions about him. You really begin to experience his grace, or the joys of being his child. You develop a sense of calm in your life. That is what we hear the apostle Peter saying. He seems to say knowing God is a source of our spiritual conviction, it is the source of our spiritual credit and it is also the source of our spiritual calm.

Knowing God is A Source Of Our Spiritual Conviction (1)

Knowing God is a source of our spiritual conviction. Listen to how verse 1 begins: "Simon Peter, a servant and apostle of Jesus Christ: To those who through the righteousness of our God and Savior Jesus Christ have received a faith as precious as ours." Let me re-word that phrase for you. It really says: To those who have received a faith as precious as ours through our God and Savior Jesus Christ." He is writing to believers scattered throughout the world, and that includes you and me. It is as if he is saying, "to those who have received a confidence as precious as ours through Jesus Christ," or "to those who have received a belief as precious as ours through Jesus Christ," or "to those who have received a conviction as precious as ours through Jesus Christ." You have a deep conviction that Jesus Christ is God. Your conviction, your confidence, your belief, your faith comes from Jesus Christ, our

God and our Savior. In other words, your faith is based on Jesus. It is not based on any other source.

A certain individual was having a conversation with his friend, and pretty quickly the conversation turned to the question of faith. The individual asked his friend, "Supposing you were to die today, are you sure you would go to heaven? In other words, if you were to die today, and were to stand before Jesus, and he were to ask you, 'Why should I let you enter my heaven?' what would you tell him?" The friend said, "Well, I went to church every Sunday. I sang in the choir. I tithed faithfully." To which the individual said, "None of those answers will do, my friend. So, the friend asked him, "Well, what about you. If you were to die today, and you were to stand before God, and he were to ask you, "why should I let you enter my heaven?', what would you tell him? He said, "Oh! I would tell him, 'It is because I know you personally as my Lord and Savior who died on the cross for me.' That is the basis of my conviction that I will enter heaven.'"

Your entry into heaven is not based on the fact that you were raised in a Christian home. Your entry into heaven is not based on the fact that you came to church regularly. Your entry into heaven is not based on the fact that you tithed regularly. Your entry into heaven will be based on the fact that you know the Lord Jesus Christ, and received him into your life as your personal Savior. That is the basis of your faith. That is the basis of your conviction. And if you have not taken the step of believing that Jesus died for you and asked him to enter your life, let me encourage you to do so. Why? Because knowing God is the basis of your conviction.

Knowing God is A Source Of Our Spiritual Credit (2)

Knowing God is not only the source of your spiritual conviction, it is also the source of your spiritual credit. The Bible says, "Grace and peace be yours in abundance, through the knowledge of God and of Jesus our Lord." Let us look at that word "Grace." Grace is receiving spiritual benefits, which neither you nor I deserve to receive from God. Grace is receiving spiritual credit which neither you nor I deserve to receive from God.

How many of you have ever had a bank overdraft penalty slapped on your account, or a late payment penalty slapped on your telephone bill, or hefty fees imposed on your credit card bill? Have you ever gone to the bank, or the telephone company, or the credit card company and asked them to waive the fee for any reason and you, miraculously succeeded?

Something like that is what happened to you and me when we believed in Jesus Christ. You must first of all admit that you are a sinner and nothing you can do will save you. But if you go to God and tell him, "Please waive the penalty for my sin. I admit I have failed you. I admit I have not lived righteously before you. Please forgive me for my sin," God will forgive you, and he will write your name in the book of life. That is grace. Sad to say this, but we have walked away from this truth. God can't wait to give you the spiritual credit of his grace. But you must ask for it. You must go to him and ask for forgiveness. We have walked away from this truth. We have walked away from this teaching. Knowing God is a source of spiritual credit.

Knowing God is A Source Of Our Spiritual Calm (2)

Knowing God is a source, not only of our spiritual conviction, or of our spiritual credit, but also of our spiritual calm. That very sentence says, "Grace and peace be yours in abundance through the knowledge of God and of Jesus our Lord." In other words, may your knowledge of God give you peace. May your knowledge of God give you serenity. May your knowledge of God give you restfulness. May your knowledge of God give you repose. May your knowledge of God give you spiritual calm. Colossians 1:20 says Jesus Christ made peace through the blood of his cross.

Have you ever noticed the difference between how a Christian suffers and how a non-believer suffers? The expressions of grief among the Hindus, for example, is an expression of utter hopelessness as they cremate their loved ones because they do not know whether they will ever see the person again, or whether that person will come back in the next life as a lower state animal. Albert Camus, the Algerian philosopher, insinuated that since life is meaningless, suicide seems to be the only option.

But the believer in Jesus Christ knows that God is the source of their spiritual calm. We are at peace because we have an anchor in Jesus Christ. We are at peace because we know that no matter what befalls us, Jesus will fix it in the long run. We are at peace because we know that death does not have the last word for you and for me. We are at peace because we know that Jesus has the last word for you and for me. We are at peace because we know that Jesus will come to our defense at the judgment seat of Christ. Knowing God is a source of spiritual calm.

Conclusion

I know you know about Jesus. You can tell me facts about him. You can describe what he did, how he did it, and when he did it. But that is not enough. You need to have a personal relationship with him, just like you have a personal relationship with your spouse, just like you have a personal relationship with your siblings, just like you have a personal relationship with your children, just like you have a personal relationship with your friends. But it is a much deeper relationship because he is not only related with you by virtue of his blood shed on the cross for you. He is also related with you because he also lives within you. Your body is his temple, and he wants to ensure that his sanctuary is holy, and righteous, and pure, and glorious. Do you know Jesus as the source of your spiritual conviction, as the source of your spiritual credit, and as the source of your spiritual calm? Have you surrendered your life to him? If you have not, why not do it today? How you respond to this question will matter for all eternity. Be sure to surrender your life to Christ. Have you done so? I pray you answer in the affirmative.

Chapter 19

Sample Sermon Three
(Preached in An Actual Conference)

Introduction

LET ME BEGIN BY acknowledging all the pastors in this conference tonight. Our organization, KCFA, values you immensely, and we are so delighted you are with us. You are an important part of our fellowship and without your spiritual guidance, KCFA would not be where it is. Thank you, every servant of the Lord, for joining us tonight. This is your organization.

Our theme this year is taken from Haggai 1:8: "'Go up into the mountains and bring down the timber and build the house, so that I may take pleasure in it and be honored,' says the Lord." This is how we are going to mark our thirtieth anniversary.

As we focus on that theme let me begin by saying this past year has been a tough one. Organizing this conference has been tough. Leading KCFA has been tough. The tendency to throw in the towel has been strong. Feeling like giving up has haunted me like you would never imagine. The demands have been overwhelming—not to mention the fact that as I speak with you, my sister who follows me is preparing to bury her husband in Kenya.

We just buried another brother-in-law in April, just when the department of women concluded its annual national departmental conference. So I am in mourning as I speak to you tonight.

When I think of all these, I ask myself, is it worth it? Should I be in this? Are we not better served if we all packed up our bags and focused on what we believe matters? After all, this is a volunteer ministry. Who wants to break his back, or break her back, volunteering for something that does not seem to pay?

Why, for example, should we even have the audacity to ask you to give toward building the retreat center? Why should we ask everyone to focus on the theme of going up the mountain and bringing down the timber and building the retreat center so that God could take pleasure in it and be honored? Why, oh, why should we venture into such an undertaking? It is a mammoth project. Should we not just throw in the towel? Should we not just walk away from this? Should we not just give up?

But when you think about it, giving up is not an option. Throwing in the towel is not an option. Something bigger than what we see is here. Something greater than what we perceive is here. We do not do this for an earthly reward. If we did this, we *would* have given up a long time ago. If we did this, we *should* have given up a long time ago. Let me tell you, that we do this because of what awaits us on the other side. We do what we do to win the crown indestructible, to win the crown of rejoicing, to win the crown of righteousness, to win the crown of life and to win the crown of glory.

We Do What We Do to Win the Crown Indestructible (1 Corinthians 9:25)

We do what we do to win the crown indestructible. Listen to what 1 Cor 9:25 says: "Everyone who competes in the games goes into strict training. They do it to get a crown that will not last; but we do it to get a crown that will last forever." What is the Bible saying here, and what is this crown that the Bible talks about? This crown is for those who win the Christian race. It is for those who live the Christian life successfully. It is for those who walk the Christian walk victoriously. It is for those who pray persistently. It is for those who fast frequently. It is for those who seek God sincerely.

When we have an over-night prayer vigil, they are there. When it is church time, they are there. They bathe their minds with Scripture. They feed their souls with worship. They dip their spirits in prayer. In short, they live the Christian life victoriously. Insults don't shake them. Gossip does not discourage them. Malice does not deter them. They keep their eyes on the crown indestructible, the crown imperishable, the crown eternal. We do what we do to win the crown indestructible.

I have heard many things in my ministry in KCFA that could have killed my spirit. If words could kill, I would be dead by now. I have been insulted. I have been disrespected. I have been ridiculed. But why do I do what I do? I do what I do because I want that indestructible crown. I want that crown that lasts forever. I want that crown that God has prepared for me.

As I was preparing this sermon today, I got some troubling news—news I was not prepared to hear and news I did not want to hear. I knew the enemy was attacking. I picked myself up and said, "This is not getting into me. Greater is he that is in me than he that is in the world."

You will be discouraged serving the Lord. You will feel slighted. You will feel let down. People will put words in your mouth, words you never said. People will read intentions into your actions, intentions you never had. Someone will put you in the same camp with the devil just because you disagreed with them. The temptation to defend yourself can be strong. The temptation to seek revenge can be strong. The temptation to get even can be strong.

Don't you lose hope. Don't you lose faith. Don't you lose your commitment. An insult is one more jewel in your crown. A disparaging remark is one more jewel in your heavenly crown. An abuse is one more jewel in your heavenly crown. The more you get the insults, the brighter your crown will shine. The more you get abused the more glamorous your crown will be. Do what you have always done in the ministry because you will win the crown indestructible.

We Do What We Do to Win the Crown of Rejoicing (1 Thessalonians 2:19)

We do what we do not only to win the crown indestructible. We also do what we do to win the crown of rejoicing. Listen to how the apostle Paul describes it in 1 Thess 2:19: "For what is our hope, our joy, or the crown in which we will glory in the presence of our Lord Jesus when he comes? Is it not you?" Paul led the Thessalonian Christians to faith in Jesus Christ. For doing so, he knew God had prepared the crown of rejoicing for him. The crown of rejoicing is the soul-winner's crown.

It is the crown Jesus has prepared for the evangelist. It is the crown you will receive for leading that brother to Jesus Christ. It is the crown you will receive for leading that sister to Jesus Christ. It is the crown you will receive for leading that child to Jesus Christ.

I don't know how true this story is, but I understand that the late Billy Graham, that great American evangelist, dreamed he died and went to heaven, and Jesus Christ was giving him his reward for the great work he had done. He received a huge prize from Jesus. The lady standing next to him, however, received an even bigger prize. So, Billy asks Jesus, in that dream, "Why did she receive a prize that is bigger than mine? I have led millions of souls to Christ. Why would she receive a bigger and better prize than mine?" And Jesus said, "The reason for that is because while you were preaching, she was praying for you. Because she spent time on her knees praying for you, many were won to Christ."

Brothers and sisters, everything you do for the sake of winning souls to Christ will matter eternally. Don't give up praying for the salvation of your child. Don't give up praying for the salvation of your spouse. Don't give up praying for the salvation of your parents. But, oh! Yes! Go out there and tell them about Jesus. Go out there and proclaim the word of God. Support the mission by going. Support the mission by praying. Support the mission by giving. Our retreat center will be a place for evangelism and discipleship. Support that mission by giving toward that cause. When you support God's mission by actually preaching, or actually praying, or actually funding it, you will receive the soul winner's crown. It is the crown of rejoicing. It is the crown of the evangelist. We do what we do to win the crown of rejoicing. That is the reason I accepted to lead KCFA—to win the crown of rejoicing. That is the reason we are in the middle of building the retreat center—to win the crown of rejoicing. It is not about what we will gain on this earth. It is about what we will receive in heaven.

We Do What We Do to Win the Crown of Righteousness (2 Timothy 4:8)

We do what we do to win the crown indestructible. We do what we do to win the crown of rejoicing. We also do what we do to win the crown of righteousness. In 2 Tim 4:8, Paul describes it as follows: "I have fought the good fight. I have finished the race. I have kept the faith. Now there is in store for me the crown of righteousness, which the Lord, the righteous judge, will award to me on that day—and not only to me, but also to all who have longed for his appearing." Paul was expecting to receive this crown because he had lived faithfully for God. He had fought the fight faithfully. He finished the race faithfully. He kept the faith faithfully. Because of that, he knew God reserved the crown of righteousness for him.

This crown is for those who live obediently for God. It is for those who confess their sins immediately they discover they have sinned. It is for those who remain faithful to God. They love the Lord so much that they do not wish to sin against him. But they love the Lord so much that when they sin against him, not only are they grieved by their sins, they repent immediately. They repent at once. They want to fight the good fight and win. They want to run the race to the finish. And they wish to keep the faith without adulteration.

A certain group of people was preaching right here in the United States. It was something like a tent revival. As the praise and worship team was singing its head off, a gentleman in the crowd that gathered to listen approached one of the members and said: "You all are here preaching the gospel and telling us about Jesus being able to cleanse us from sin. But let me tell you one thing: There is a difference between having your sins washed white, and having them whitewashed." Always strive to have your sins washed away completely. Don't settle with having your sins whitewashed. Strive to finish your race well.

Several years back, when we moved to Florida, we met up with the gentleman that taught me a course called "Old Testament Survey," and this happened at Scott Theological College in Machakos, Kenya. As I sat there with him, he very pointedly looked at me and said, "You know something, Joseph. My biggest concern in life, and my greatest ambition in life, is to finish the Christian race well. I want to finish well."

It is one thing to begin the Christian race strong. It is quite another to finish strong. Don't begin strong and finish poorly. That is what we see in quite a number of the Old Testament kings. Solomon started well but finished poorly. Asa started well but finished poorly. Uzziah started well but finished poorly. Joash started well but finished poorly. Josiah started well but finished poorly. Start well and finish well. Start strong and finish strong. Start in the power of the Holy Spirit and finish in the power of the Holy Spirit. When you do, you will receive the crown of righteousness promised you by God. You will stand next to the apostle Paul receiving that crown of righteousness. We do what we do to win the crown of righteousness.

We Do What We Do to Win the Crown of Life (James 1:12)

We do what we do to win the crown indestructible. We do what we do to win the crown of rejoicing. We do what we do to win the crown of righteousness. But we also do what we do to win the crown of life. Listen to the word of God in Jas 1:12. It reads: "Blessed is the man who perseveres under trial, because when he has stood the test he will receive the crown of life that God has promised to those who love him."

When you persevere under your trials, when you withstand your tests, you will receive the crown of life. When you prevail under persecution, when you triumph over tribulation, when you conquer your crises, you will receive the crown of life. The crown of life is meant for those who overcome their spiritual obstacles, who defeat their spiritual dangers, who conquer their spiritual crises.

Shortly after my wife was diagnosed with breast cancer, I remember asking her whether I should step down from the presidency of KCFA in order to take care of her. I could not stand the fact that she was dealing with such a deadly disease, and yet I was needed to travel all over the country to encourage the chapter members of KCFA. I told her I was ready to submit my resignation letter immediately. She said, "Don't you dare do it! This is my battle. You have a different battle to fight. Fight that battle and finish it."

At that moment, the words of James came to mind. "Blessed are you when you persevere under trial, because when you stand the test, you will receive the crown of life." You know what that meant to me. If I stepped down at that time, I would not have withstood the test, and I would not have been eligible for that crown. I would have put myself in a position of losing that crown. You don't want to lose that crown.

Do you feel like giving up serving the Lord? Do you feel like throwing in the towel and not praying as you should or worshiping as you should or going to church as you should, perhaps because of some sickness in your family, or because of some trial in your church or because of some persecution at your workplace or because of some hatred from your Christian brother or because of some challenges in your finances or because of some unexplainable reason? Don't! Don't give up! Don't give in! Don't surrender! Don't yield! Your crown of life is waiting for you. Your crown of life is at the finish line. Your crown of life is coming soon. As long as God gives me breath, I will take this KCFA presidency to the finish line because I want that crown of life. We do what we do to win the crown of life.

We Do What We Do to Win the Crown of Glory (1 Peter 5:1-3)

We do what we do not only to win the crown indestructible, or the crown of rejoicing, or the crown of righteousness or the crown of life. We also do what we do to win the crown of glory. The Bible says in 1 Pet 5:3: "And when the chief shepherd appears, you will receive the crown of glory that will never fade away." This crown is for pastors. If you are a pastor listening to this sermon, this crown is for you. But you must fulfill several conditions to win this crown. The conditions are listed in verse 2. It says, "Be shepherds of God's flock that is under your care, serving as overseers—not because you must, but because you are willing, as God wants you to be, not as greedy for money, but eager to serve, not lording it over those entrusted to you, but being examples of the flock."

Condition number one: you must *serve willingly* to win the crown of glory. Condition number two: you *must not be greedy for money* to win the crown of glory. Condition number three: you must *be eager to serve* to win the crown of glory. Condition number four: you must *not be like a slave-driver who lords it over your flock* if you want to win the crown of life. Condition number five: you must *show a good example* if you want to win the crown of glory.

This is not just for the pastor who takes care of the flock in an official church. It is for you who must pastor your children. It is for you who must lead a Bible study. It is for you who provide spiritual guidance and direction of some kind to those you care about. This crown is for you who must help counsel someone out of a crisis.

A certain pastor showed up for his new job disguised as a homeless person. He wore dirty clothing. He was dressed in tatters. He looked unpresentable. He walked into the church through the door like everyone else. No one wanted to greet him. No one wanted to shake his hand. No one wanted to talk to him. The only person who knew what was happening, was the elder who led the worship service that morning. When he introduced the new pastor, imagine the shock and horror on people's faces when he stood up in front of them all and said, "Hi, I am your new pastor. And today, I am going to talk to you about showing kindness and love to strangers." The sermon that day was very uncomfortable.

Sometimes, dear pastors, you will have to preach uncomfortable sermons. Sometimes you will have to make uncomfortable decisions. Sometimes you will have to make painful corrections in the lives of those under your care. Sometimes you will be unpopular. Many times you will be misunderstood. Many times you will be misinterpreted. You will be discouraged. You will feel defeated. You will feel vanquished. Don't give up. A crown of glory is awaiting you. A crown of glory is in store for you. A crown of glory has been reserved for you. It is more precious than an Olympic gold medal. It is more glamorous than an Oscar. It is brighter than a Super Bowl ring. It comes with the glory of heaven, adorned with celestial beauty, sealed with divine fingerprints, glittering with eternal brilliance, endowed with infinite value, and conferred upon you by the King of kings, and Lord of Lords, when he returns in majesty and splendor. I want that crown. That is why we do what we do—to win the crown of life.

Conclusion

But the real reason I do what I do is because Jesus died on the cross for me. The real reason I do what I do is because I was lost, but now I am found. I was blind, but now I see. I was heading to destruction, but Jesus saved me when he died on that cross. If he gave his life for me, it is not too much for me to live for him. If he gave his life for you, it is not too much for you to live for him. And that is why we ask you to go up the mountain, bring down the timber and build a house for him so that he may take pleasure in it and be honored. I believe it is one way of winning that crown. We do what we do to win the crown indestructible, to win the crown of rejoicing, to win the crown of righteousness, to win the crown of life and to win the crown of glory.

And when you get to that universal homecoming, you will see that crown for what it is: I will call it the ABCs of your heavenly crown. It is an attractive crown. A beautiful crown. A celestial crown. A delightful crown. An elegant crown. A flamboyant crown. A glamorous crown. A heavenly crown. An illustrious crown. A joyous crown. A kingly crown. A lucrative crown. A magnificent crown. A numinous crown. An outstanding crown. A prepossessing crown. A quintessential crown. A riveting crown. A stellar crown. An unadulterated crown. A vintage crown. A wondrous crown. A xesturgic crown. A Yahweh-given crown. A zestic crown.

I wish I could describe that crown! You just have to be there to see it. But to be there, you must surrender to the lordship of Jesus Christ. But to surrender to the lordship of Jesus Christ, you must say Lord, forgive me. I am a sinner. Enter my heart. Write my name in the book of life. Today I am yours. And he will make you a citizen of heaven with the rights and privileges thereof.

Index